Jesus

He's all you'll ever need

Jesus

He's all you'll ever need

Mike Tucker
of Faith for Today

Pacific Press® Publishing Association
Nampa, Idaho
Oshawa, Ontario, Canada
www.pacificpress.com

Book designed by Eucaris L. Galicia
Cover photo copyright by GoodSalt.com

Copyright © 2005 by
Pacific Press® Publishing Association
Printed in the United States of America
All rights reserved

Additional copies of this book are available by calling toll free
1-800-765-6955 or visiting **AdventistBookCenter.com**

ISBN: 0-8163-2112-4

05 06 07 08 09 • 5 4 3 2 1

Contents

Introduction

"There is not a heart but has its moments of longing, yearning for something better, nobler, holier than it knows now" (Henry Ward Beecher).

Does your heart long for something better? My heart certainly does. Somewhere deep inside I experience a gnawing sense that I am incomplete and need to be made whole.

It has been my experience that houses, cars, clothes, money, vacations—even a new or improved life do not satisfy my longing. I and countless others have tried to satisfy the desire, but all our efforts have proven to be inadequate. This struggle isn't unreasonable or hard to understand. If the source of the longing is difficult to identify, then certainly the solution should be equally illusory. And on those rare occasions when we seem to catch a hint of exactly what it is for which we are longing, we're not certain we want to accept the cure.

Christian author George Macdonald understood this dilemma. He wrote: "Man finds it hard to get what he wants because he does not want the best; God finds it hard to give because He would give the best, and man will not take it." Macdonald's statement makes me think of an ill child who refuses to take the medicine prescribed for his illness. While Mom holds the spoon of liquid, the child clenches his jaw in firm resolve to refuse the cure. And so he suffers on.

But the medicine Jesus offers is not some foul-tasting syrup. The cure He offers is sweet and easy to swallow.

I have learned, through bitter experience, that my heart's desire can be satisfied only through a deep, meaningful relationship with a person. Not just any person. There is one specific Person who alone satisfies my longing heart. That Person is Jesus.

This book is an attempt to demonstrate that Jesus can satisfy the desire of every heart. I have attempted to demonstrate this fact through a study of Jesus' life. The best source material for such a study can be found in the four Gospels of the New Testament. I have focused my attention on Luke's Gospel. It is my fervent hope that you will discover, as you read, what countless others have found through the centuries—that Jesus is your heart's desire.

When I first experienced the fulfillment of my heart's longings, my life was changed! I was inexorably drawn to Jesus. I understood what Charles de Foucald had written so many years before: "The moment I realized that God existed, I knew I could not do otherwise than to live for Him alone." For me, it wasn't just an acknowledgment that God existed, but that He was approachable! I learned that He was the kind of God with whom I could feel safe—the kind of God I could even enjoy. When I saw that, I knew that I must live for Jesus alone!

It is my prayer that if you have not yet found this kind of God, or if you are in need of a richer understanding of His love, this study of Luke's Gospel will reveal Him to you in the person of Jesus of Nazareth. If you already know the fulfillment of heart-longings that a relationship with Jesus provides, then perhaps this book will serve as confirmation of what you already have experienced to be true. Whatever your experience, I pray that God will bless you abundantly as you read of Jesus, your heart's desire.

Mike Tucker

Chapter One

What Is Your Heart's Greatest Desire?

Based on Luke 1; 2

A young man who was suffering from depression went to a renowned doctor in Paris. This young man was desperate! He desired to be happy—to have the longing in his heart satisfied. He would do anything the doctor told him to do if only it would fill the void in his life!

In those days there were no such things as antidepressants, so the doctor had to be creative. He thought of a well-known young man, Grimaldi, who he considered might serve as an example for the sad young man in his office. Grimaldi was a playboy, one of the beautiful people who enjoyed a rich night life in Paris; he was known for his lighthearted attitude. So the doctor's prescription for the depressed young man was this: "Introduce yourself to Grimaldi. Let him show you how to enjoy yourself, and you will get well."

To the doctor's surprise, the young man's pain appeared to increase when he heard the wise prescription. With a downcast spirit, he said, "I am Grimaldi."

Do you, like Grimaldi, feel that something is missing in your life? Are you ever in search of something—anything—to make you feel complete?

Look up the word *desire* in any thesaurus and you'll find synonyms such as "hunger," "longing," and "yearning." What all these words express is an almost desperate sense that something is missing.

When I first realized this longing in my own heart, I was desperate to fill the emptiness I felt. As a young boy, I attempted to fill the longings of my heart with sports. I played sports; I watched sports on television; and long after my parents thought I was fast asleep, I listened to sports on the radio. I loved the Dallas Cowboys. I admired Sandy Koufax of the Dodgers. And I longed to play basketball like Connie Hawkins. But sports failed to make me feel any better about myself.

Later in life, music served as a substitute for genuine wholeness in my life. I embraced everything from Brahms to the Beatles. I learned to play musical instruments and sang in groups. Although the joy of music temporarily lifted my spirits, the longings remained unfulfilled.

As adolescence bloomed, I attempted to fill the void in my heart with a fascination for the opposite sex. Thoughts of girls filled my days and my nights, but still left me empty.

Some older, well-intentioned people who were watching my struggles suggested to me that I was spending too much time on things that didn't matter. They said that my love for sports, music, and girls was the problem.

Larry Crabb disagrees with their well-intended criticisms of my life. He wrote, "The core problem is not that we are too passionate about bad things, but that we are not passionate enough about good things."

My preoccupation with sports, music, and girls was not the real problem in my life. It was a symptom of a deeper, greater problem. The problem lay at the core of my being, and it affected everything about my life. The problem left me with a deep desire for something more—something that would finally complete me. I was not too passionate about sports, music, and girls! I just was not passionate enough about my heart's true desire.

What is it that your heart desires more than anything else? What is your greatest longing?

Even the happiest and most successful people, when pressed, will often admit that something is missing, that something is not quite right.

Somehow we sense that we were made for more than we are experiencing, that we were intended to live better than we do.

Perhaps even Sylvester Stallone would admit that something is missing in his life. Stallone is a successful movie star. By the time he was thirty-five he had starred in three successful hit movies—*Rocky, Rocky II,* and *Rocky III.* But then Stallone's world fell apart when his three-year-old son, Seargeoh, was diagnosed with autism.

"When I heard, I was violently angry," Stallone said. "I didn't understand why this would happen to my boy. I felt betrayed. If you have a bad hand to deal, God, give it to me, not to an innocent child. What purpose did it serve? Was my life too good? Is it something I did, some word I said? Seargeoh has no idea who I am. I'm just another person to him. You have to accept his love on his terms. There is nothing I can offer or buy or give my son that can help him. I feel I let my child down. I feel helpless, and I have to accept that."

The limitations of fame and fortune became apparent in Sylvester Stallone's life when this tragedy struck. The man who had it all realized that all wasn't enough when it came to his son's autism.

Is there some sadness in your life? Is there some void, some emptiness, that nothing seems to be able to fill?

Somewhere deep inside, something tells you that it was not intended to be this way. Your life was not meant to be like this. You were destined for more!

When I was twelve years old, my parents took me to New York City. Understand, I was no country bumpkin, but New York blew me away! Although I had grown up in Fort Worth, Texas, and had made numerous trips to Dallas, I was unprepared for what I saw in New York. I marveled at that spectacular city with its museums, galleries, and concert halls. I couldn't quite get over the tall skyscrapers. I wondered how it was possible to make something that tall. I couldn't imagine how much money it took to build all those structures. New York City cried out to me of financial success and abundance.

And yet, in the midst of all these wonders, my eyes fell on a shabbily dressed woman who was rummaging through garbage cans, desperately looking for something to eat. My mother saw me staring at the woman, put her arms around me, and said, "God loves her, too, Mike. She is one of His creatures."

Today, as I think about that woman, I wonder about her when she was a child. What had her mother and father hoped and dreamed for her when she was born? Wasn't she intended for something other than a life spent scrounging through garbage cans in an attempt to survive?

The same is true for us. Our lives may have somehow fallen far short of the hopes and dreams we embodied when we were born. We intuitively sense that we were intended for something greater—something more.

At the heart of these feelings of incompleteness is a gnawing fear that the problem actually lies within us! As much as we may want to blame society, the government, our boss, our spouse, or our parents, we eventually come back to the sickening fear that the real problem lies with us. That, in fact, we are to blame. We are haunted by the sense that we are flawed, that we are not good enough, not smart enough, not skilled enough, or that we are so inferior as to be completely unlovable.

Author Donald Miller, in his book *Blue Like Jazz,* wrote, "I think every conscious person, every person who is awake to the functioning principles within his reality, has a moment where he stops blaming the problems in the world on group think, on humanity and authority, and starts to face himself. I hate this more than anything. This is the hardest principle within Christian spirituality for me to deal with. The problem is not out there; the problem is the needy beast of a thing that lives in my chest" (p. 20).

Could it be true that the problem lives within us?

Feelings of incompleteness and longing are not new. They didn't originate with this generation. They are nearly as old as the planet. The Bible tells us that they originated with our first parents, Adam and Eve.

After Adam and Eve broke their perfect relationship with God, their hearts were filled with fear. They hid themselves, hoping that God would not find them. But God went looking for them, and found them. And when He found them, it was obvious that these once-perfect beings were seriously flawed.

If Adam and Eve feared that their longings were the result of their being flawed, they were right! Their sin had separated them from the only true Source of fulfillment—God. Before their sin, Adam and Eve enjoyed face-to-face friendship with God. But because of sin's propensity to separate us from God, their sin made such intimacy with God impossible for them. God planted seeds of longing in the hearts of Adam and Eve—a longing for what they had lost—a longing to see God face to face.

Every son and daughter of Adam and Eve has inherited that same longing, that desire to be restored to what we were made to be. I've got it, and most likely, you've got it as well. And as long as you have it, you will not be satisfied.

Helen Keller said it best: "One can never consent to creep when one feels an impulse to soar." We were made to soar, and until we do, we will never be whole. But the good news is that God sees our longing. The better news is that He has done something about it.

The very first day that Adam and Eve experienced a longing in their hearts through their own disobedience, God announced a plan to satisfy that longing. We find the announcement in Genesis 3:15. Using highly symbolic language to announce His plan, God spoke directly to Satan:

> "And I will put enmity
> between you and the woman,
> and between your offspring and hers;
> he will crush your head,
> and you will strike his heel."

Satan is at war against God, and therefore, he is at war with the woman and her offspring. In Bible prophecy, a woman represents the church, so her offspring would represent the members of the church, believers, down through the ages. Basically, anyone who longs for fellowship with God could be included in this group.

Satan is at war with everyone who feels a longing for closeness with God. He fights that war by attempting to separate human beings from intimacy with God. But the prophecy states that Jesus would bring the war to a victorious climax by crushing Satan's head. In the process, however, Jesus would also suffer a wound, described as a wound to His heel. This refers to the death of Jesus on the cross. A wound to the head is fatal; a wound to the heel is not. Jesus' death on the cross was not permanent. He died, but He rose again. On the cross Jesus made the ultimate sacrifice so that He might once and for all win the war against Satan.

Why was He willing to go to all that trouble and all that pain and expense to redeem a rebellious planet? He was willing because the day that Adam and Eve broke their relationship with God, God felt something new! God's great heart began to ache! God missed the friendship He had with Adam and Eve.

God felt a longing in His heart—a longing to restore Adam and Eve, as well as all their descendants, to that which they were intended to be. Adam and you were intended to be God's friend, and God is lonely for you!

All of us—everyone who ever has or ever will live on this planet—were intended to know uninterrupted, unimpaired friendship with God. When Adam's sin altered that friendship, God longed for the friendship to be restored. So Jesus volunteered to come and make the supreme sacrifice. It would cost Him greatly. But it was a sacrifice He was willing to make because it was the only way to fulfill the longings of His great heart! It was the only way to restore you to what you were meant to be, what you were created to be—God's friend!

This is the desire of God's heart, and it is the desire of your heart as well. It is the desire to see and to know God. Jesus is the embodiment of that desire because He is the only way our heart's desire will ever be fulfilled.

For centuries, true followers of God listened to the prophets who foretold the arrival of One who would fulfill their heart's desires. A Jewish priest, Zechariah, and his wife, Elizabeth, were people with such longings. First, this couple longed for the promised One who would fulfill the desires of every heart. Secondly, this older, childless couple longed for a child!

One day when Zechariah was serving in the temple, he went in to burn incense in the temple. But what happened next left Zechariah dumbfounded—literally—as we shall see. Luke tells the story in his Gospel: "Then an angel of the Lord appeared to him, standing at the right side of the altar of incense. When Zechariah saw him, he was startled and was gripped with fear. But the angel said to him: 'Do not be afraid, Zechariah; your prayer has been heard. Your wife Elizabeth will bear you a son, and you are to give him the name John' " (Luke 1:11–13).

At first sight, only one of the prayers prayed by Zechariah and Elizabeth was to be answered—the prayer for a son. But when the angel began to speak of the work that this son would accomplish, it became clear that a second prayer was to be answered as well. A few verses later, the angel announces the role of their son who was to be born: " 'And he will go on before the Lord, in the spirit and power of Elijah, to turn the hearts of the fathers to their children and the disobedient to the wisdom of the righteous—to make ready a people prepared for the Lord' " (verse 17). Zechariah's son was to prepare the way for the One who would satisfy the desires of every heart. His son would lead the way for the Messiah. His was to be a work of preparation.

Zechariah asked how all of this would come about since he and Elizabeth were old. His question was cynical, a question of disbelief in the angel's promise. It is as though he were saying, "Yeah, sure! Like that's going to happen! Do you realize how old we are? Don't you know how long it has been since our honeymoon?" The angel rebuked his disbelief by telling him that he would be struck dumb until the child was born.

Zechariah left the temple and came to those who were waiting and praying outside. When he tried to speak, he was unable to say anything, and he remained that way until after the child was born.

On the eighth day of the child's life, as was the custom, Zechariah and Elizabeth took the boy to the temple to be circumcised and to have his name registered. When asked what the child's name would be, Elizabeth answered that it was to be John. It was the custom in those days to name a child after someone in the family, but there was no one by that name in their family. The priests turned to Zechariah, who wrote on a tablet, "His name is John." At that moment, Zechariah was able to speak again, and the first words he said were praises to God. Luke records Zechariah's song of praise:

> "Praise be to the Lord, the God of Israel,
>   because he has come and has redeemed his people.
> He has raised up a horn of salvation for us
>   in the house of his servant David" (Luke 1:68, 69).

Later, we find Zechariah speaking of his son, John:

> "And you, my child, will be called a prophet of the Most High;
>   for you will go on before the Lord to prepare the way for him,
> to give his people the knowledge of salvation
>   through the forgiveness of their sins" (Luke 1:76, 77).

John was to prepare the way for the One who would supply the longings of every heart! He would prepare the way for the One who would make it possible for us to have face-to-face friendship with God. This One would remove the impediments to intimacy with God by providing for the forgiveness of our sins.

Through the pages that follow we are going to study the Gospel of Luke in an attempt to learn about Jesus. And what we will discover is this: Jesus is your heart's desire. Jesus is your opportunity to know God and to see Him face to face.

God understands the desires of your heart—perhaps even better than you do. He understands that you feel incomplete, as though you really don't belong. But God is determined to heal your brokenness and satisfy your longings. That is why He sent His Son. Jesus came to fulfill your heart's desire.

To everyone today who feels that he or she is somehow incomplete, I say that you are not alone and your case is not hopeless! Jesus came to satisfy the longings of your heart. He came to forgive your sins, to make it possible for you to know God. You were made for fellowship with God. You may try to fill your emptiness with many things, but none of them will last or be ultimately fulfilling.

A young boy growing up in west Tennessee had identified in his own heart a burning desire for something more, something better. He lived in an extremely poor family. He came from "the wrong side of the tracks."

Someone had given him an old, secondhand guitar. His cousin, country singer Lonzo Green, came to visit the family. During his visit he taught the boy a few basic chords. A love for music grew in the boy's heart as he spent many happy hours playing and singing.

Whatever became of that boy? You know him as Elvis Presley, the King of Rock and Roll. His music affected the industry for decades.

However, as exciting as his "rags to riches" story is, wealth and fame could not satisfy the deepest longings of Elvis's heart. Through the years he developed addictions to alcohol and drugs, struggled with his weight, and struggled with depression. He died a rather inglorious death and forever stands as an example of a failed attempt to fulfill the heart's longing with anything but Jesus.

Only friendship with Jesus will satisfy. You were made for fellowship with God.

Perhaps today's most respected theologian, John Stott, wrote in *The Contemporary Christian,* "Our greatest claim to nobility is our created capacity to know God, to be in personal relationship with him, to love him and to worship him. Indeed, we are most truly human when we are on our knees before our Creator."

As you read the Old Testament, you realize that the greatest desire of the prophets was to see God face to face. But since sin entered the planet, no one was allowed to look into the face of God. For the Hebrews, to say that you gaze into someone's face is to say that you know them well—intimately as two great friends. This is the experience that Adam and Eve had before they sinned, and it is the experience that the Old Testament writers longed for—to gaze directly into the face of God.

The Hebrew benediction illustrates this:

> " ' "The Lord bless you
>   and keep you;
> the Lord make his face shine upon you
>   and be gracious to you;
> the Lord turn his face toward you
>   and give you peace" ' " (Numbers 6:24–26).

This passage illustrates Hebrew parallelism. The same thing is said in three different ways. The statements the Lord "bless you," "make his face shine," and "turn his face toward you" are three ways of saying the same thing. May you gaze into the face of God—may you know Him in the ultimate face-to-face relationship.

This was the type of relationship Adam and Eve had before they sinned, and it is the type of relationship we crave today. This is the longing of every heart.

God experiences longings as well—longings for restoration of face-to-face friendship with you. And so God took the initiative and pursued you through His Son, Jesus.

Luke tells us that a young girl named Mary was anxiously awaiting the fulfillment of the prophecies regarding the One who would satisfy the longings of every heart. Mary was betrothed to a man named Joseph. A betrothal was something more than an engagement and something less than a marriage. It was a binding contract of marriage. In those days most girls were married between the ages of twelve and sixteen, so we can assume that Mary was very young when she was promised to Joseph.

Before her wedding day, Mary received a visit from an angel: "God sent the angel Gabriel to Nazareth, a town in Galilee, to a virgin pledged to be married to a man named Joseph, a descendant of David. The virgin's name was Mary. The angel went to her and said, 'Greetings, you who are highly favored! The Lord is with you.' Mary was greatly troubled at his words and wondered what kind of greeting this might be. But the angel said to her, 'Do not be afraid, Mary, you have found favor with God. You will be with child and give birth to a son, and you are to give him the name Jesus' " (Luke 1:26–31). Mary asked how this would happen since she was unmarried and a virgin. Mary's question was very different from the one asked by Zechariah. Zechariah was cynical about what the angel had promised, but Mary assumed that what the angel had said would take place—and wondered how it would all come about. The angel's answer is found in verse 35: " 'The Holy Spirit will come upon you, and the power of the Most High will overshadow you. So the holy one to be born will be called the Son of God.' " This Baby was to be the One who was promised by prophets of old. He would satisfy the longings of every heart.

Mary did indeed become pregnant, even though she was a virgin. God planted the fetus inside Mary, and when it was obvious that she was pregnant, Joseph considered ending the engagement. According to Jewish law he could have had Mary put to death, but he decided just to send her away instead. That is, until he, too, was visited by an angel.

The angel told him of the unique circumstances of Mary's pregnancy, and Joseph began to understand that this was to be a very special baby. So Joseph did not send Mary away. And when he had to go to Bethlehem to pay his taxes, Mary accompanied him. There in Bethlehem, Jesus was born in a stable.

As strange as was the pregnancy of his wife-to-be, Joseph somehow realized that something special was happening in the birth of this Child. Broken people were to be made whole. Joseph began to understand that this was the reason for Jesus' arrival on earth. This Baby was God, pursuing us so that He might make the weak strong, the diseased healthy, the incomplete complete, and the broken whole. It was God coming to restore us to what we've never been but have always known we were intended to be.

Christian author Ravi Zacharias, in his book *Recapture the Wonder,* tells of a friend who was in France, visiting the famous Louvre art gallery. While there he saw a group of blind students who were taking a tour of the gallery. It seemed incomprehensible that blind children should visit an art gallery! But as he watched, he saw that their tour guide took pains to describe each painting in great detail.

Then the children were taken to another room where the ancient statue of a Greek Olympic athlete stood on a pedestal. Each child, guided by the teacher, was allowed to touch the statue. Their hands traced the powerful body, the perfect physique of the athlete.

Then some of these skinny kids started to feel each other's thin arms and giggled at the difference. Their faces gave them away as they wondered what it must be like to have a physique like that of the athlete's. But there was also the thought that they should become that person—that they were intended to be someone with not just an athletic body but with eyes to see and a life worth living.

Most of us often feel like those kids. We know we are not what we were intended to be. We long for someone to come and restore us to what we have never been but always should have been. That Someone is Jesus. Blind children discovered this through the beauty of art.

Speaking of such beauty and the longings of the soul for something better, Christian author C. S. Lewis wrote more than sixty years ago: "We do not merely want to see beauty, though, God knows, even that is bounty enough. We want something else which can hardly be put into words—to be united with the beauty we see, to pass into it, to receive it into ourselves, to bathe in it, to become part of it. . . . At present, we are on the outside of the world, the wrong side of the door. We cannot mingle with the splendors we see. But all the leaves of the New Testament are rustling with the rumor that it will not always be so. Some day, God willing, we shall get in."

Some day, we shall get into heaven, and there we will see God. Because Jesus was willing to make such a huge sacrifice, we will one day have all our longings satisfied. One day we will see God face to face!

You recall, once more, the story of Adam and Eve when they sinned. They recognized their sin and hid themselves from God. When Adam and Eve hid themselves, what did God do? He looked for them and called to Adam, "Adam, where are you?"

It wasn't that God didn't know where Adam was, but He wanted Adam to know that He was looking for him. He wanted Adam to understand that God knew the longings Adam and Eve were experiencing—He understood their feelings of desire. He knew because he was experiencing something similar. God longed for renewed friendship with Adam and Eve.

But it was God who sought the first couple, not they who sought Him. God took the initiative. He didn't allow Adam to hide. He came searching for him. God took the initiative to restore their friendship even while Adam was hiding.

He has done the same for you. Long before you acknowledged or understood the longings of your heart, God began the search for you. He took the initiative by sending Jesus. Jesus came to restore intimacy and fulfill the desires of your heart. He is the One whom Isaiah, Zechariah, Elizabeth, Mary, and Joseph all longed so see. And He is the One your heart longs for. Even when you don't recognize it, He is the One who can make you whole. Jesus is your heart's desire.

Chapter Two

When Do You Feel Most Loved?

Based on Luke 5:17–26

An elderly, wealthy gentleman married a lovely young lady who was many years younger than he. Shortly after the wedding he wondered whether she might have married him just for his money. The possibility left him feeling unloved. So in a tender moment he broached the question: "If I lost all my money, would you still love me?"

She said reassuringly, "Oh honey, don't be silly. Of course I would still love you. And I would miss you terribly."

Not exactly the reassurance the old guy was looking for, was it?

When do you feel most loved? When is it that you know for certain that you are truly loved?

Luke tells the story of a man who really did feel loved—not just by his friends, but also by God. In this story, Jesus has traveled to the town of Capernaum and is most likely staying and teaching in Peter's home. Luke says, "One day as he [Jesus] was teaching, Pharisees and teachers of the law, who had come from every village of Galilee and from Judea and Jerusalem, were sitting there. And the power of the Lord was present for him to heal the sick. Some men came carrying a paralytic on a mat and tried to take him into the house to lay him before Jesus" (Luke 5:17, 18).

The fact that the paralytic in this story had friends suggests that at one time he had been able to walk. If he had been born this way most people would have shunned him because they viewed such infirmities as a direct punishment from God for sin—perhaps the sin of the parents. But this man had friends, friends who came to know and love him before he had lost mobility.

In those days, when a man became paralyzed, he had very few options. There was no Social Security system, no welfare, no insurance, and no way for such a person to earn a living. The chances were excellent that such a person would starve. Most working people lived on the edge of hunger because a day's wages was just barely more than it took to feed a family. So there was not a lot of disposable income for people to feed someone who couldn't work. The only option left was to beg for whatever money one might receive from sympathetic passers-by on the street.

To add to this humiliation, the religious leaders of the day told such people that they had gotten exactly what they deserved. The priests told this man that his paralysis was God's punishment for some sin he had committed. They told him that he was an evil person whom even God could not love. So this man's helplessness and physical pain were complicated by feelings of rejection, guilt, and shame.

As much as he longed to be healed and to walk again, quite possibly he longed even more to know that God could love and forgive him. His heart longed to be restored to a relationship with a God who loved him. But this man was fortunate beyond measure. He had friends who wouldn't let him give up. They were willing to do anything necessary to help their friend.

One day they learned that this new Teacher, Jesus, had come to their town, Capernaum. Already stories of Jesus' miraculous power over sickness had circulated. Immediately they thought of their beloved, paralyzed friend. These four friends went to the home of the man they loved as a brother and told him of their plan. They would take him to the Healer and ask Him to heal their friend.

Perhaps the man resisted. Perhaps he was too embarrassed, or too depressed to entertain hope. But his friends persisted.

Most poor people in those days slept on a small straw mat that usually lay on the floor. The four friends attached ropes to the four corners of the man's mat, hoisted the ropes over their shoulders and carried him through the city streets. They carried their friend to the house of Peter. Peter was now a full-time follower of Jesus and was out of town most of the time. Jesus was staying at Peter's house, and when the people discovered that He was there, they pressed around the house to hear Him preach.

Jesus was standing inside the house, just inside the front door. The door was open, and Jesus preached to the people who were inside the house and also to those who had pressed close to the front door on the street outside. There were so many people there that the four men who carried their friend couldn't get to the front door. They tried over and over again, but to no avail. But they weren't about to give up!

In those days, houses in that part of the world had flat roofs and a stairway on the back of the house that led to the roof. In the cool of the evening, families would go to the roof and sit there enjoying the evening together before they retired. These four men carried their friend to the back of the house and climbed the stairs to the roof. They laid the man down and then estimated where Jesus must be standing in the house. Then they began to tear up the roof!

Houses were usually rectangular in shape and had beams that stretched across the breadth of the structure spaced about three feet apart. The beams were covered with palm branches, tiles, and mud. The mixture was allowed to dry in the hot sun. The result was a fairly solid roof.

These men started to rip up the tiles, the mud, and the palm branches in order to get through to Jesus! Eventually, people became distracted by the commotion. Dust and debris began to fall around Jesus until He finally had to stop preaching and watch with amusement as the roof opened and the sun shone through.

By this time, no one was listening to Jesus preach. They were all focused on the commotion happening on the rooftop. Jesus had to interrupt His teaching and join the crowd in watching this comic opera unfold.

At last, one of the men stuck his head through the hole, then pulled it back up and said to his friends, "We found the right spot!" The men continued digging to make the opening larger. When the hole was big enough, these four determined men took the ropes that were attached to the four corners of their friend's bed and lowered him into the house, right at Jesus' feet. It was an amazing sight—almost comical! The paralyzed man lay at the feet of Jesus, looking up into His face.

What must that moment have been like for this man? I'm certain that he looked up in anticipation—but anticipating what? Remember that his experience with religious leaders had been disastrous. These religious leaders had told him that he was a sinner and deserved his paralysis. That his physical problems were God's wrath being poured out upon him.

The paralytic felt the stinging rebuke of the religious leaders, and in his mind, it was the rebuke of God. He felt he was someone whom God could never love. And he didn't know if Jesus would do the same thing—reject him as defective, disgusting, and sinful!

But the man was paralyzed! He couldn't escape the tension of this moment. He had to lie there and wait to see what Jesus might do. This paralyzed man was entirely at the mercy of Jesus.

However, his fears were allayed when he saw the look in Jesus' eyes. He saw something there he had not seen with the religious leaders. He saw a look of compassion, a look of love.

If you had been standing where Jesus stood, what would you think as you looked down at this paralized man on his mat? What would you imagine this man could possibly want? What would you guess was the reason such great efforts had been made to bring him to you?

The most obvious thing was that he must want to be healed. He must want to be able to walk again, to work again, to have restored mobility. That was what everyone assumed who was watching this drama unfold. They all anticipated that healing was the great heart's desire of this paralyzed man. However, his disability may not have been the primary thing on his mind.

I have noticed that often those we think of as being disabled have greater wisdom than most people. You see, they've been forced to think about life and its meaning. And quite often what they find is that their disability is not the worst thing that has ever happened to them. I've even met some who were thankful for their disability because of what it had taught them about life. One man said to me, "I've come to realize that I was paralyzed long before my accident. My paralysis was of mind and of spirit."

In a very real sense, all of us have a disability. Our disability results from our separation from God. It has created a longing in our heart—a desire to be restored to friendship with God. The longing to be with God is almost overwhelming.

We see a reflection of this longing in our eagerness just to be in the presence of people we love. Often, we go to great lengths to feel the love of family and friends.

Alvin Straight longed to see his brother. When Alvin was seventy-four, his brother, Henry, suffered a stroke. Alvin was desperate to see his brother, but his poor eyesight prevented him from driving. So Alvin did something completely unexpected. He drove his lawn mower from Iowa to his brother's house in Blue River, Wisconsin, a distance of 240 miles!

The trip took a month and a half. Alvin attached a trailer to his mower to carry gasoline, clothes, food, and camping gear. Alvin did all of this because he loved his brother and wanted to spend some time with him.

Alvin died on November 12, 1996. His funeral procession included family members pulling a trailer with a lawn mower on top as a tribute to Alvin's love for his brother. That love and the longings it created drove Alvin to desperate measures.

As a pastor, I see this longing in the faces of men and women every day. They may approach me with a problem, but the problem they present is not always the real problem. The real problem is their longing for God.

Eugene Peterson, writing to pastors, wrote, "More often than we think, the unspoken, sometimes unconscious, reason that persons seek out conversation with the pastor is a desire to keep company with God."

Certainly, Jesus understood this to be true. He saw that this was the true, secret desire of the paralyzed man. But something complicated that man's longing. It was the nagging, gnawing sense that separation from God was his own fault and that God was angry over the separation. Would God's anger prevent him from ever keeping company with God?

Deep inside, all of us, like the paralytic, sense that the separation is our fault. We realize that our sin keeps us from God, that our failure has prevented us from becoming all that we were intended to be. Many of us carry around a load of guilt, a feeling of unworthiness. These feelings can be debilitating.

Psychiatrist Carl Jung mused that 90 percent of his patients in the psychiatric hospital could go home if they could know that they were forgiven. Perhaps the same was true with the paralytic in Luke 5. Jesus must have sensed it. He must have seen what others could not see.

Everyone else who looked upon that scene saw a man with withered, atrophied arms and legs. They could see only the disability, and they fairly cried out for Jesus to heal the man so that they wouldn't have to look on him with pity. But Jesus was able to look past the exterior disability and see the man's real disability. He saw the crushing sense of guilt and rejection this man felt. He saw the deepest longings of this man's heart.

So Jesus did something quite unexpected. "He said, 'Friend, your sins are forgiven' " (verse 20).

What a curious thing to say! Everyone who stood there watching this drama thought they knew what the man really wanted. He wanted to be healed, to be able to walk again.

But Jesus saw the man's real need; He saw the deepest longings of this man's heart. And Jesus dealt with the most important disability first. He told this man that his sins no longer stood between him and God.

Jesus came to reconcile sinful men and women to God—to restore them to the relationship they were created to experience. And Jesus announced to this man that no longer was there a barrier between him and God. The friendship was restored! He was forgiven!

And Jesus called the man "friend"! If Jesus was who He claimed to be, the Son of God and therefore, Deity Himself, then it was God who called this broken refuse of humanity "friend." God called the paralyzed man whom religious leaders had judged and found guilty "friend"!

This man knew something of what it meant to have friends. Four men had proven themselves to be the best friends anyone could ever hope to have. But now Jesus claimed to be the man's Friend as well. He was implying that there were no limits to His friendship; that He would stop at nothing to fulfill the desires of this man's heart.

The same is true for you. Because Jesus came to this world, the very thing that separates you from God can be swept away. Your sins can be forgiven. Jesus can see past the exterior of your life, gaze deeply into the core of your being, and see your true need. It matters not what you have done. Christ is anxious to forgive you today and to call you His friend. Just as He forgave this paralyzed man, so too, does He forgive you! Jesus loves you and proves it today by forgiving your darkest sin.

An Indian proverb states, "A guilty conscience is a hidden enemy." This was certainly true of the paralytic, and it may also be true of us. But Jesus defeated our hidden enemy. He defeated that enemy when He won the right to forgive our sins on a cruel cross.

Even though the paralytic had experienced rejection from the religious leaders of his day, he would not have the same experience with Jesus. When his friends laid him at the feet of Jesus, his heart's greatest desire was first revealed—and then fulfilled. Jesus looked at the paralytic, saw his heart's greatest desire, and then announced to that man that his sins were forgiven.

The wall of separation between the paralyzed man and God had been torn down by grace. The paralytic was loved, accepted, and forgiven by God.

Jesus' words had an immediate effect on the man. When He said, "Friend, your sins are forgiven," those words immediately changed that man's life completely.

Malcolm Muggeridge wrote, "Psychiatrists require many sessions to relieve a patient of guilt feelings which have made him sick in body and mind; Jesus' power of spiritual and moral persuasion was so overwhelming that he could produce the same effect just by saying: 'Thy sins be forgiven thee.' "

I believe at that moment—the moment Jesus announced the forgiveness of this man's sins—he was ready to go home. I believe he felt he could live with paralysis if only he knew that God loved him.

Do you realize how valuable that is? When we come to Jesus we have a means of getting rid of our guilt. We have the forgiveness of Christ!

Theologian John Stott wrote, "A leading British humanist was interviewed recently on television. In a moment of surprising candor, she said, 'What I envy most about you Christians is your forgiveness. I have nobody to forgive me.' "

What the humanist had learned was that even in her "godless" world, guilt was a fact of life. If there is no God, what do you do with your guilt? Who or what releases you from feelings of guilt? If there is no One to absolve you, then you must continue to carry your guilt throughout time in a godless universe.

But we do have someone to forgive us! Jesus forgives our sins today. And so I believe that when the paralytic experienced the forgiveness of Christ, he was ready to go home. He was ready to go home because his greatest need had been met—his sins had been forgiven, and he knew that God loved him deeply. To this man, walking was not nearly as important as knowing he was accepted in the presence of God.

However, as always, there were doubters in the crowd. The religious leaders of the day were not happy. Look at what happened next: "The Pharisees and the teachers of the law began thinking to themselves, 'Who is this fellow who speaks blasphemy? Who can forgive sins but God alone?' " (verse 21). Luke says that the Pharisees were thinking—not speaking, but thinking—that Jesus was a blasphemer. Blasphemy is the sin of claiming to have rights, powers, or authority that belong only to God. If Jesus were a mere mortal, He would have been guilty of blasphemy by claiming to forgive sins. But Jesus was not just a man. He was also uniquely God. And, as God, Jesus knew what these men were thinking.

"Jesus knew what they were thinking and asked, 'Why are you thinking these things in your hearts? Which is easier: to say, "Your sins are forgiven," or to say, "Get up and walk"? ' " (verses 22, 23). Don't you imagine that a cold chill went up and down the spine of these men when Jesus let them know He knew what they were thinking? Think of the panic of knowing that their deepest, darkest thoughts could be read by this man!

These were the doubters, the naysayers! They had worked hard to deny that their hearts even had longings. Now they were intent on making certain that no one else would have their longings satisfied either.

But Jesus wasn't about to allow doubters to undo what He had just accomplished. He took a rather curious tactic to defeat their assault on the work of grace. He asked a question that, on the surface, seemed rather insignificant. He asked whether it was easier to say, "Your sins are forgiven" or to say, "Get up and walk."

Truthfully, if you do not want to be exposed as a fraud, it is much easier to say, "Your sins are forgiven," because no one can prove that you are wrong. But if you say, "Get up and walk" and the man doesn't walk, everyone knows you are a fraud.

I imagine that Jesus paused after He asked this question to let the full significance sink in. And then Jesus increased the stakes. He issued a direct, in-your-face challenge to the doubters: " 'But that you may know that the Son of Man has authority on earth to forgive sins . . . ' He said to the paralyzed man, 'I tell you, get up, take your mat and go home.' Immediately he stood up in front of them, took what he had been lying on and went home praising God. Everyone was amazed and gave praise to God. They were filled with awe and said, 'We have seen remarkable things today' " (verses 24–26).

"To prove to you that I have the authority to forgive sins, watch this!" Jesus said to the doubters. Then He commanded the man to get up and walk—and he did exactly that! Atrophied arms and legs were suddenly strong and straight. The man stood on strong legs, rolled up his bed with strong arms, and walked through the crowd. The men who had mentally accused Jesus of being a blasphemer now had to step aside as the paralyzed man walked past. Those who had refused to let him through so that he could get to Jesus had to step aside to let him walk out!

Jesus performed two miracles that day. The first miracle was an inner, unseen miracle. It was the forgiveness of sins. No one could prove it had actually happened. Then Jesus performed a second miracle. The second miracle was outward, visible, and undeniable. The second miracle proved that the first miracle had really taken place!

Just so, Jesus performs two miracles in the life of every man, woman, and child who come to Him today. First, He forgives your sins, thus restoring you to intimacy with the Father. His forgiveness takes away the guilt and the shame. He takes hold of you and lifts your life out of the slime and crud of sin. Jesus shatters your shame by cloaking you in His love. He repairs the brokenness of your life, sweeping away that which is inferior and replacing it with His own perfection. This is the first, invisible miracle.

Then, to prove that the first miracle has taken place, Jesus performs a second, visible miracle. He changes your life! Jesus makes you a different person—one who resembles Jesus Himself. Day by day, Jesus changes your attitudes and behaviors so that others might take note that something special has happened to you. You have been changed from the inside out!

Just as Jesus performed two miracles in the paralytic, He also performs two miracles in you. He forgives your sins, and then He changes your life.

This is a love that is relentless! What more could Christ do to prove His love for you? You were separated from Him by your sin. Perhaps you have felt the longing in your heart for a restored relationship with Jesus. Jesus feels it, too, because He misses the intimacy of your friendship. So Jesus took the initiative, came to earth as a baby, paid your penalty, and thereby won the right to forgive you and reconcile you to God.

But He doesn't stop there. Jesus goes the second mile and changes your life so that you actually look, think, and act like Jesus Himself. He does all of this to prove His love for you!

When do you feel most loved? For me, it's when I know I have been forgiven, accepted, and loved by my God! It is then that I know I've experienced God's relentless love—a love that will not let me go. It is a love that longs to forgive me, restore me, and change me.

A while back I came across the story of a mother whose heart was breaking over the rebellion of her teenage daughter. It seemed as though they did nothing but fight! The long struggle between mother and daughter hit its all time low when the young girl was arrested for driving under the influence of alcohol.

After posting bail for her daughter, the mother did not speak to her daughter until the next afternoon. When they came together, she handed her daughter a small, wrapped gift. The girl flippantly opened it and was exasperated by what she saw. The box contained a small rock. She rolled her eyes and asked, "What's this for?"

Her mother simply replied, "Read the card."

She did and was overcome by the words inside. Tears began streaming down her cheeks as she reached out to embrace her mom.

The card said, "They tell me that this rock is more than a million years old. That's how long it will take before I give up on you." (*Bits & Pieces,* July 16, 1998, p. 16.)

Do you think that rebellious teenage girl felt loved at that moment? Her mother's unrelenting, forgiving love broke through to her hardened heart. Her mom looked past the exterior of an angry, petulant teenager and saw a little girl who longed to be loved, accepted, and forgiven. She saw her daughter's greatest need and lovingly supplied it. And what do you want to bet that that love eventually worked in the girl's life to change her?

When do you feel most loved? For me, that's easy. It is when I've experienced the forgiveness of God for my sins. I know I am loved when by the power of His gracious love, Jesus changes my life to resemble His holy life.

Two miracles occur in my life. The first is hidden—no one sees it. I am forgiven. The second gives evidence that the first has indeed taken place. My changed life is proof that Jesus loves and forgives me. When that happens, I feel loved.

Mitsuo Fuchida was a staunch military pilot who led the attack on Pearl Harbor. He was a proud Japanese warmonger who admired Adolf Hitler. He wore his hair like Hitler and sported the same little mustache.

Fuchida took part in the Battle of Midway, the Marianas Turkey Shoot, and other major engagements of the Pacific war. He stood on the deck of the USS *Missouri* at the surrender ceremonies. Though defeated, he was pleased with his behavior as a pilot.

After the war, though, he became disillusioned. He was surprised to learn that Japanese POWs were treated humanely—in sharp contrast to the Japanese treatment of Allied prisoners. He also learned of a woman who ministered to the Japanese prisoners. Her parents were missionaries to Japan but had been beheaded by his countrymen. She had forgiven the Japanese and met the needs of their captured soldiers.

Such love led Fuchida to the Bible. He eventually became a Christian and later an evangelist. Before his death in 1976, he led many to Christ through his preaching in Japan and the United States.

Mitsuo Fuchida experienced two miracles. The first was when he accepted the forgiveness of Christ for his sins. The second was when Jesus changed his life to more closely resemble His life. That was when Mitsuo Fuchida felt loved!

That's when I feel loved. Wouldn't you like to feel that kind of love today? If so, pray this simple prayer with me today:

Dear God, something seems to be missing in my life. I feel empty, alone, unfulfilled, and hopeless. The Bible suggests that my feelings of inadequacy are the result of my sin—the result of the fact that I, of my own power, cannot do right.

In Your Word You tell me that if I will admit that I am a sinner and ask to be forgiven of that sin, You will do just that—You will forgive me. It also says that when You forgive me, You will also remove the wall that separates me from You and allow me to feel complete, whole, fulfilled.

God, in faith, I confess my sins today. I humbly ask for Your forgiveness. And just as surely as I have asked, I now receive. I give You thanks for forgiving my sins.

I further ask that You would grant me an experience of closeness with You. I'm not even certain what that means, but I'll trust You to reveal it to me.

And by the way, Lord, would You allow me to have that feeling of closeness throughout all eternity? You promised it in the Bible, and I, through faith, claim it today.

Thank You, God, for Your forgiveness, and for giving me the desires of my heart. Amen.

Although there is nothing at all magic about these words, if you prayed these words, or similar words, in faith, you were forgiven that very moment. The longings of your aching heart are about to be satisfied. Trust the One who never rejects you. You are about to discover what it feels like to be truly loved!

Chapter Three

What Is the Best Gift You've Ever Received?

Based on Luke 7:36–50

In January 2004, Kevin Shelton went to the mall in Tampa, Florida. Kevin had strapped wads of cash to his body with the plan of giving it all away. In two hours, the thirty-two-year-old man gave away seven thousand dollars, one dollar at a time. The recipients of the gifts rewarded Shelton with smiles, hugs, and "thank you's."

Shelton made his money buying and selling real estate in the Tampa area. Most shoppers took the money and walked away giggling. Some recipients said they would give the money to someone in need. Shelton says a few people actually scolded him for not giving the money to the truly needy.

Shelton began giving away cash in an attempt to bring cheer and spark generosity. He says, "I think it's making an impact." Although Kevin doesn't keep track of how much he gives away, his best guess is that he has passed out tens of thousands of dollars.

What's the best gift you've ever given someone? Or, let's ask that question the other way around. What's the best gift you've ever received?

In Luke's Gospel we find a story of gifts that were given and received:

> Now one of the Pharisees invited Jesus to have dinner with him, so he went to the Pharisee's house and reclined at the table.

When a woman who had lived a sinful life in that town learned that Jesus was eating at the Pharisee's house, she brought an alabaster jar of perfume, and as she stood behind him at his feet weeping, she began to wet his feet with her tears. Then she wiped them with her hair, kissed them and poured perfume on them (Luke 7:36–38).

Matthew tells this same story in his Gospel, and he includes the fact that the Pharisee who invited Jesus to have dinner in his home was called Simon the Leper.

Leprosy was a dread disease in those days, a disease with no cure and that was always fatal. Because leprosy was contagious, lepers were forced to live apart from family and friends. By law, they could have no contact with anyone and had to warn those who might come near by screaming "Unclean! Unclean!" at the top of their lungs. Simon had contracted the disease, but Jesus had healed him. Now Simon wanted to express his gratitude by throwing a dinner party. Jesus gave Simon the gift of being healed, and Simon gave Jesus the gift of a dinner party.

The woman spoken of in this passage had not been invited to the party. She was a woman of poor reputation. Several Bible scholars accept the tradition that identifies this woman as Mary Magdalene, who was also the sister of Martha and Lazarus. It has been further suggested that she was the victim in the story of the woman caught in adultery (see John 8).

Scripture tells us that Jesus had, on seven different occasions, cast demons out of Mary. Since we know that she had worked as a prostitute, and since even today prostitutes almost always have addiction problems, we are safe in assuming that at least some of the demons Jesus cast from Mary were demons of addictions. Perhaps they were sexual addictions, and almost certainly addictions to substances.

Not only had Jesus delivered Mary from these things, He had also forgiven her and accepted her. Jesus had given Mary gifts of incredible value. Jesus gave Mary the gift of freedom from addictions, as well as the gifts of forgiveness, dignity, and self-respect.

Mary's heart was overflowing with love toward Jesus. She longed to give Him something in return. But what could she possibly give to match the incredible gifts she had received?

Mary's sister, Martha, had been hired by Simon to prepare the special dinner for Jesus. This is how Mary learned of the gathering and how she gained access to Simon's home. Simon was a Pharisee, and therefore a religious leader in the community. Mary was a woman with a bad reputation. Simon would never have allowed Mary to enter his home for any purpose whatsoever! But Mary gained access to Simon's home through her sister, Martha.

Mary bought a very precious and costly perfume, one that would have cost the equivalent of a year's wages for an average worker. In a day when women were not allowed to own property or run a business, how did Mary come by such a large sum of money? No doubt she earned the money while working as a prostitute. Mary used the money earned from her illicit trade to buy a present for the Son of God! Her unholy income purchased a gift of love for the One who is entirely holy. And wonder of wonders, Jesus accepted the gift!

Truthfully, what gift can any of us give to Jesus that is not somehow tainted? Our lives are unholy messes; our best efforts so much worthless garbage. In fact, that is exactly what Isaiah says:

> All of us have become like one who is unclean,
>   and all our righteous acts are like filthy rags;
> we all shrivel up like a leaf,
>   and like the wind our sins sweep us away (Isaiah 64:6).

In reality, what Isaiah said was not nearly as polite as that which is printed in our English versions of Scripture. The "filthy rags" were menstrual cloths, a form of refuse made even more undesirable by the Jewish ceremonial laws. Anyone who touched such an item would be prevented from entering the temple. A period of cleansing along with a special ceremony were required to make the "defiled" individual eligible for readmittance to temple worship.

Isaiah said that all of our very best acts are polluted. The very best we have to offer Christ is disgusting refuse. Therefore, it is only God's grace that permits Him to accept our offerings. That grace is so rich that it can make even a gift purchased by the illicit profits of prostitution into something so wonderful that we celebrate it as a beautiful offering of love.

If God's grace was strong enough to do this for Mary's gift, it can do the same for your offerings of love as well. Your life may not be everything it should be, but you must never allow that to keep you from approaching Jesus. Jesus' grace will turn even the most crass offerings into something of beauty and genuine value. His grace is sufficient for you!

Mary was an uninvited, unwanted guest in Simon's home. How would she be able to approach Jesus with her gift? Mary had a plan. She would simply creep in during the meal, pour the contents of the box on Jesus' feet, and then slip out unnoticed.

In those days, people didn't sit at a table to eat like we do today. They reclined on couches, propping themselves up with one arm while they ate with the other hand. Their head would be at the table, and their feet would be away from the table. Therefore, Jesus' feet would be accessible to Mary.

Women did not eat with the men. They served the men, and then, after the men had eaten, the women would eat in another room. So after the meal had been served and all the men were engaged in conversation and in eating, Mary came in with the perfume.

But Mary's plan had a few flaws. First, she had forgotten to bring a towel to wipe the excess ointment from Jesus' feet. And second, she had forgotten just how pungent the fragrance would be. When she opened the box, the sweet aroma filled the entire room. The diners could smell it above the aroma of the food they were eating. Soon, everyone knew that something was going on.

As Mary thought about what Jesus had done for her, she began to weep. When she realized her mistake in not bringing a towel, she let her hair down and began to wipe Jesus' feet with her hair. This was social suicide for Mary because no respectable woman ever revealed her hair in public. The hair was always kept up and then covered with a headdress. But Mary removed the headdress, let down her long hair, and used it to dry Jesus' feet. It was a terribly intimate thing to do and was very embarrassing for everyone present.

Luke tells us of Simon's discomfort with Mary's act: "When the Pharisee who had invited him saw this, he said to himself, 'If this man were a prophet, he would know who is touching him and what kind of woman she is—that she is a sinner' " (verse 39).

Jesus had healed Simon, but Simon was not yet a believer. He still had questions about Jesus, and when he saw this rather embarrassing situation in which Jesus allowed a woman of bad reputation to perform such an intimate act on His feet, Simon was certain that Jesus couldn't be from God! Jesus knew what Simon was thinking, and so, He engaged him in conversation.

> Jesus answered him, "Simon, I have something to tell you."
> "Tell me, teacher," he said.
> "Two men owed money to a certain moneylender. One owed him five hundred denarii, and the other fifty. Neither of them had the money to pay him back, so he canceled the debts of both. Now which of them will love him more?"
> Simon replied, "I suppose the one who had the bigger debt canceled."
> "You have judged correctly," Jesus said (verses 40–43).

The principle Jesus is teaching here is this: The person who has been forgiven more will love more. The greater the debt that has been forgiven, the greater the love given in return! Simon was uncomfortable with Mary's unseemly behavior. But Jesus said that it was perfectly understandable in light of the enormity of the gift she had been given—the gift of forgiveness.

But I find a problem here.

Truly, Mary had received an extravagant gift. She had been forgiven of great things and had been loved and accepted just as she was. Mary knew she was a sinner and knew that Jesus had pulled her back from a great precipice and saved her. And for this she was eternally grateful.

However, correct me if I'm missing something here, but hadn't Simon received a gift of great value as well? Leprosy had signed Simon's death certificate! Not only was the disease fatal, but as soon as Simon was diagnosed, he became a social outcast, unable to fellowship even with his own family! Jesus had not just saved Simon's life, He had restored the man to social acceptability! He returned the man to the arms of his wife and children—returned him to his friends, his work, his home, his way of life!

Mary had been forgiven, and her life changed, but she was still a social outcast—a fallen woman who was not welcome in Simon's home for a dinner party! Hadn't the gift Simon received been at least as great as the gift Jesus gave to Mary? Couldn't it be argued that Simon had received the more complete gift? And yet, Mary was the one whose gratitude had resulted in an appropriate response.

Is it possible that Jesus was giving Simon a gentle hint? Well, if a gentle hint wasn't enough, Jesus next leaves the world of gentility and moves right up to "in your face"! "Then he [Jesus] turned toward the woman and said to Simon, 'Do you see this woman? I came into your house. You did not give me any water for my feet, but she wet my feet with her tears and wiped them with her hair. You did not give me a kiss, but this woman, from the time I entered, has not stopped kissing my feet. You did not put oil on my head, but she has poured perfume on my feet. Therefore, I tell you, her many sins have been forgiven—for she loved much. But he who has been forgiven little loves little' " (verses 44–47).

Now we understand! As great as was the gift Jesus had given to Simon, it was not as great as the gift He gave to Mary. The greatest gift is never physical healing nor restoration of respectability and social status. The greatest gift is forgiveness. We learned this when we looked at the story of the paralyzed man in Luke 5. Jesus forgave the paralytic before He healed him, and the man was ready to go home even without being healed, as long as he knew he was forgiven. Mary had been forgiven, but Simon had been only healed! And the greater of the two gifts is forgiveness.

Forgiveness is the greater gift because to be forgiven is to be saved for eternity. To be forgiven is to have opened to you the possibility of face-to-face friendship with God. Have you received the greatest gift? Have you been forgiven?

What is the greatest gift you have ever been given? It is the gift of forgiveness.

Bob Hoover was a famous test pilot and a frequent performer at air shows. Once, while flying his plane home after an air show in San Diego, both engines of his World War II propeller plane suddenly stopped. With skill and a lot of luck, he safely landed the plane without injury to himself or the two passengers. After the emergency landing he inspected the airplane's fuel. As he suspected, the plane had been filled with jet fuel rather than gasoline.

He then asked to see the mechanic who serviced his plane. The mechanic, horrified at the prospect of seeing the man he had nearly killed, anticipated the full force of Hoover's anger. But Hoover put his arm around the mechanic and said, "I'm sure you'll never do this again. And to show you how sure I am of that, I want you to service my P-51 tomorrow." Now that's forgiveness, and forgiveness is the greatest of all gifts!

Simon had received a great gift as well. Simon had been healed of leprosy and restored to his family as well as to his position in society. Because of his gratitude, he opened his home and threw a dinner party for Jesus.

Throwing a dinner party is a nice gesture, isn't it? But it is not an overwhelming response. After all, Jesus had rescued Simon from a slow, agonizing death. Jesus had restored him to his family, his position in the community, and to respectability. So, for Simon to throw a dinner party was certainly not too extravagant a response.

On the other hand, Mary had been forgiven. Mary's life had been one of prostitution and addictions. Jesus rescued her from this life and forgave her sins. Jesus had not restored her reputation; she was still a social outcast—a fallen woman. But Jesus rescued her and forgave her.

It is a great thing to receive physical healing, but Jesus demonstrated that it is a better thing to be forgiven. Mary had received that greater gift, and so Mary's response of gratitude threw caution to the wind. She forgot about propriety and forgot about thrift. She took the money she had saved from her illegitimate trade and spent a year's wages on a gift of her gratitude. She emptied the contents of the alabaster box just as she poured out all the love she felt for Jesus. Mary held nothing back. She gave it all to the One she loved.

Mary wept as she kissed Jesus' feet and wiped them with her hair. It was unseemly, embarrassing, and extravagant, but most of all, it was the only appropriate response. While it is a great thing to experience physical healing, it is a far, far greater thing to be forgiven, loved, and accepted!

Jesus pointed out the difference in the two responses: "Then he turned toward the woman and said to Simon, 'Do you see this woman? I came into your house. You did not give me any water for my feet, but she wet my feet with her tears and wiped them with her hair. You did not give me a kiss, but this woman, from the time I entered, has not stopped kissing my feet. You did not put oil on my head, but she has poured perfume on my feet. Therefore, I tell you, her many sins have been forgiven—for she loved much. But he who has been forgiven little loves little' " (verses 44–47). On the surface it appeared that Simon was honoring Jesus with the dinner party, but in reality, he had not taken the whole thing seriously. It was a grave insult for a man of position and wealth to invite someone into his home and not provide a servant to wash the feet of the guest. People wore open-toed sandals and walked on dusty, unpaved roads. Feet were always dirty. Therefore, it was the custom to have a servant greet guests with a bowl of water to wash their feet as they entered the house. Simon had not done this. It was a detail he would not have overlooked if he had been serious about honoring his Guest.

Mary didn't wash Jesus' feet with water; she washed them with tears and kisses. She didn't wipe them with a towel, but with her hair!

Long hair was the pride of every woman in those days. Women didn't cut their hair, and they didn't show their hair in public. Women kept their heads covered in public. A woman would uncover her hair only in private with her husband. But Mary let her hair down in public and then used it as a towel.

It was the custom to greet an honored guest with oil and to anoint his head as a gesture of blessing and refreshing. But Simon had not done this for Jesus.

Mary, on the other hand, anointed Jesus with precious perfume. The contrast could not have been greater! Mary recognized the value of the gift she had received, while Simon did not. And because Mary recognized the value of the gift, she loved Jesus greatly. " 'Therefore, I tell you, her many sins have been forgiven—for she loved much. But he who has been forgiven little loves little' " (verse 47).

Mary had many sins, but they were all forgiven, and that was why she loved Jesus so very much. Simon had been only healed. He had not been forgiven, and therefore he loved little.

Why hadn't Simon been forgiven? There can be only one reason. He didn't see that he needed to be forgiven. His heart had not been broken by his sin. Simon hadn't recognized his need and had not asked for forgiveness.

Jesus cannot forgive a sin of which you don't repent. However, just as soon as you repent, Jesus forgives. The apostle John assures us of this: "If we claim to be without sin, we deceive ourselves and the truth is not in us. If we confess our sins, he is faithful and just and will forgive us our sins and purify us from all unrighteousness. If we claim we have not sinned, we make him out to be a liar and his word has no place in our lives" (1 John 1:8–10). Simon didn't see his need and therefore deceived himself. The truth was not in him. Simon couldn't be forgiven until he admitted that he needed forgiveness. Simply put, Simon didn't feel guilty.

We usually think of guilt as being something purely negative. However, guilt is a wonderful gift from God. If we never feel guilt, we never see the need to change.

Dr. William Glasser is the father of reality therapy. Glasser says that without personal disapproval for current behavior, positive changes in behavior will never occur. What does that mean? It means that if you never feel guilty, you will never change!

Let's take Glasser's principle a step further. If you never feel guilty, you will never repent. If you never repent, you will never know the joy of forgiveness.

If you feel guilty about the mistakes of your life, rejoice! The truth has taken your heart captive! This is the first step toward repentance and forgiveness.

Mary knew that she was a sinner. There was absolutely no doubt in her mind. Her guilt plagued her; she wore it on her face every day. Mary had been the object of ridicule by "decent" women of the day. They hurled insults at her, called her names, and spat on her. But the abuse they gave Mary was nothing in comparison to the way she punished herself! Her regret was great.

Have you ever felt this way? Has your regret for mistakes been so great that you tend to constantly beat yourself up? Is your self-talk negative, filled with ridicule and statements of personal invalidation?

I have tended to follow an all too familiar pattern in my life. When I really blow it—when I do something I really wish I hadn't done—I tend to trash myself over the mistake. My self-talk is extremely negative. I find it difficult even to confess my sin before God, because I feel I'm too bad even to be in His presence. I feel so unworthy, I can't even pray.

Only after I've spent a great deal of time flogging myself over my sin do I ever come to Jesus to ask for His forgiveness.

Slowly, I am learning that Jesus is the enemy of self-hatred. Self-hatred not only is a waste of time but is actually counterproductive to the purposes of God in my life. Self-hatred destroys. Forgiveness, acceptance, and love are creative forces. God is the God of creation. Since He is still actively creating in my life, He never uses destructive forces. Instead of using self-hatred, God uses acceptance, forgiveness, and love to accomplish His purposes in my life.

Mary must have felt as though she didn't deserve to live, much less to be found in the company of decent people. That was how she felt, and that was how everyone treated her—everyone, that is, except Jesus. Jesus treated Mary as though she was pure. He treated Mary as though she were a princess.

Mary felt that her life stood in stark contrast to how Jesus treated her. But when Mary was with Jesus, she felt like "someone" rather than just "something"! She recognized the value of the gifts Jesus had given her. He had rescued her from a living hell. He never condemned her but offered loving acceptance.

Now that Mary had been discovered at the dinner party, Jesus came to her defense once again. He recognized the love this woman felt for Him—a love given in gratitude for the marvelous gift He had given her. And then Jesus spoke directly to Mary. He said, "Your sins are forgiven" (verse 48).

We heard similar words flow from the lips of Jesus as He addressed the paralytic. Jesus saw the man's greatest need and gave him the greatest gift. Jesus saw Mary's greatest need. He knew the great sorrow she felt for her sin. But Jesus couldn't just leave her there in the midst of her guilt and shame. He couldn't leave her without hope, and He wouldn't condemn her. Jesus never attacked the sinner, He simply said, "I forgive you."

A man was awakened in the middle of the night by a phone call. On the other end, a frantic, sobbing girl managed to get out the words, "Daddy, I'm pregnant." He was groggy and stunned, but he communicated his forgiveness and prayed with her. The next day he and his wife wrote their daughter two letters of counsel and love.

Three days later the man received another phone call. His daughter was shocked by the letters, because she was not the one who had called. Some other distraught girl had dialed a wrong number!

Nonetheless, the letters were not wasted. Their expressions of unconditional love and forgiveness are now a treasured possession. Here is an excerpt: "Though I weep inside, I can't condemn you, because I sin, too. Your transgression is no worse than mine. It's just different. It all comes from the same sin package you inherited through us. We're praying much. We love you more than I can say. And respect you, too, as always. Remember, God's love is in even this, maybe especially in this. This is a day of testing, but hold our ground we must. God will give us the victory. We're looking forward to your being at home. Love, Dad."

The forgiveness these parents offered when they thought their daughter was pregnant gives us just a small taste of how our heavenly Father responds to us when we sin. His loving heart rushes to forgive and to save!

With God, forgiveness of sin is absolutely necessary! Forgiveness is salvation, and salvation is forgiveness. You can't have one without the other. That is why forgiveness is such an important gift. That is why it is a greater gift than healing.

Healing just helps you live a little longer in the midst of this cruel, dark world. Eventually you will die anyway. But forgiveness fits you for heaven. It seals in you the promise of eternal life. When you are forgiven, you will live forever!

What is the greatest gift you have ever received? If you have received Jesus as your Savior, the greatest gift you have ever received is the gift of His forgiveness for your sins. Your negative past has been swept away; your salvation, secured. But just as Mary felt it necessary to respond to such love, so, too, must you.

What will you give to the One who has given you the greatest gift you've ever received? Will you give Him sweet-smelling perfume in an alabaster box? Will you give Him money, jewels, or your hard work?

Ralph Waldo Emerson said it best: "Rings and jewels are not gifts, but apologies for gifts. The only gift is a portion of thyself." In response to the love Jesus has shown you, give Him the only thing He really wants. Give Him yourself.

Chapter Four

What Do You Do When Your Life Spins out of Control?

Based on Luke 8:22–25

In his book *In the Eye of the Storm,* Max Lucado tells the story of Chippie the parakeet. Chippie's owner decided to clean out Chippie's cage with a vacuum cleaner. After removing the attachment from the end of the hose, she stuck the hose in the cage.

Everything was working fine until the phone rang and she turned to pick it up. The woman failed to pay attention to the vacuum hose, and before she knew it, Chippie got sucked in!

The woman gasped, turned off the vacuum, and opened the bag to find Chippie, still alive, but horribly shaken by his ordeal. The poor bird was covered with dust and dirt, so the woman ran with Chippie to the bathroom and held him under the faucet to wash him off! Then she remembered that Chippie was not a duck and probably was not enjoying the shower. In fact, poor Chippie was soaked and shivering. So, you guessed it, she grabbed the hair dryer and began blasting him with hot air!

Lucado wrote, "Poor Chippie never knew what hit him."

The event made it into the newspaper, so now the whole town knew about Chippie's ordeal! A few days later, the reporter who wrote the story called to check up on Chippie. The lady said, "Well, Chippie doesn't sing much anymore. He just sits and stares."

Unless I miss my guess, some of you feel a lot like Chippie today. You've been sucked into the muck and mire of life, nearly drowned in a deluge, and fairly blown away by the strong winds of strife. After all that, you probably don't sing much anymore either!

Some days it seems that life spins out of control. When that happens, how do you cope? What do you do when your life is out of control?

In chapter 8 of his Gospel, Luke tells a story of a storm and the chaos that storm created for the disciples. This story illustrates how we can handle the storms of our own lives. "One day Jesus said to his disciples, 'Let's go over to the other side of the lake.' So they got into a boat and set out. As they sailed, he fell asleep. A squall came down on the lake, so that the boat was being swamped, and they were in great danger" (Luke 8:22, 23).

In Jesus' day, most people traveled by walking. The distances between towns in Palestine were not great, and few were wealthy enough to own a horse or donkey to ride, so most people walked.

As you look at a map of Palestine you will see that the Jordan River runs north to south through the middle of the country. The Jordan feeds into a lake called Gennesaret, which is also known as the Sea of Galilee. From the Sea of Galilee, the Jordan continues its southern decent and ends in the Dead Sea. Very often people chose to travel by boat between the regions known as Decapolis and Galilee. This type of travel made the journey quicker and more pleasant than walking. So, on this particular day Jesus suggested that they travel across the lake in a small fishing boat.

Jesus was exhausted. As He felt the gentle breeze and the ripple of the water against the side of the boat, He was fairly mesmerized and fell asleep.

I've had a similar experience. Once some friends invited us to spend an afternoon on board their small sailboat. It had been a particularly busy time for me, and I hadn't had much sleep. Once on board that little boat, the warm sun, the wind on my face, and the hypnotic sound of the water against the sides of the boat produced a trancelike state. I fell fast asleep. I wasn't much company for my friends, but I had an excellent nap!

This is exactly what happened to Jesus. He was exhausted from the work of teaching and ministering to the sick. Jesus was just worn out! When the disciples pushed the boat away from the shore, the lake was so peaceful that Jesus relaxed and fell fast asleep.

But the peace didn't last for long. The Sea of Galilee is surrounded by high hills and is subject to sudden storms. The wind can whip through those ravines and make this fairly small body of water extremely tempestuous.

One of those storms swept down on that lake and stirred up the water. There the disciples and Jesus were, just minding their own business and enjoying an evening on the lake when, without warning, they got sucked into a little hurricane! Suddenly, everything was out of control. Like Chippie, the parakeet, they were sucked up by the vacuum, tossed in the dirt, held under the faucet, and blown about by a blast of hot air!

A number of years back, Pepper Rodgers was the head coach of the UCLA football team. One particular season was just miserable. UCLA couldn't seem to beat anyone! It got so bad that it even upset Rodgers's home life.

He recalls, "My dog was my only friend. I told my wife that a man needs at least two friends—so she bought me another dog."

Now that's pretty bad! Coach Rodgers's own wife was ready to fire him as head football coach!

This story is amusing, especially since it happened to someone else. But when similar episodes occur in our own lives, they are nothing to laugh about. They leave us feeling as though the entire world has turned against us. It seems that everything that could go wrong has gone wrong. Such times may come suddenly, as happened to Jesus and the disciples in the boat. Or they may develop more slowly.

Perhaps you saw the clouds gathering, then felt the wind pick up, and next you saw the first few drops of rain. You struggled, and at first it seemed as though you might actually be able to cope. But then the momentum of the storm grew until your little boat was sinking, and you couldn't bail fast enough to keep up!

That night on the Sea of Galilee, the disciples thought for a while that they might be able to handle things without disturbing Jesus.

After all, they were fishermen. They knew how to handle a boat in a storm. However, this storm became so intense that the boat began to sink!

The storms of life happen for everyone at some point. Life is just cruising along when everything goes wrong.

I know a man who thought his life was going just fine until he lost his job, watched his wife leave with his best friend, suffered as his only son rejected his values, and then learned that he had cancer. He asked me, "How am I going to cope with all that?" He had been sucked up, covered with muck, nearly drowned, and practically blown away!

I read about another man who eventually learned to cope with the storms of life. When he was seven years old, his family was forced out of their home, and he had to go to work. When he was nine, his mother died. He lost his job as a store clerk when he was twenty. He wanted to go to law school, but he didn't have the education. At age twenty-three, he went into debt to be a partner in a small store. Three years later his business partner died, and the resulting debt took years to repay.

When he was twenty-eight, after courting a girl for four years, he asked her to marry him, and she turned him down. Twice he ran for Congress and was defeated. On his third try, at age thirty-seven, he was elected to Congress, but then failed to be re-elected.

His son died when only four years old. When this man was forty-five, he ran for the U.S. Senate—and lost. At forty-seven, he ran for the vice presidency—and lost. But at fifty-one, he was elected president of the United States.

You've probably figured out that this man was Abraham Lincoln, a man who learned to face discouragement and move beyond it. How did he do it? Here's a hint.

In the midst of the Civil War, in 1863, Lincoln established the annual celebration holiday Thanksgiving Day. Lincoln had learned the secret of handling the storms of life. He learned to call out to God in the midst of trouble.

We can learn much from Lincoln's experience, and we can learn even more from Luke's story of the storm on the Lake of Galilee. After the disciples tried everything they knew, in desperation, they finally gave up on their own efforts and cried out to the only One who could help.

When the disciples realized that Jesus was sleeping through the storm, they woke Him up. "Master! Master!" they cried, "we're going to drown!" (See verse 24.)

The storm threatened to destroy the tiny boat and all its thirteen passengers. The disciples struggled with the sails; they leaned against the tiller; they rowed with all their might; they bailed for all they were worth—but to no avail! That little boat was going down!

Peter, Andrew, James, and John were all fishermen. They had seen a few storms like this before. They knew such a storm could be deadly. They had watched as the splintered remains of friends' boats had washed ashore. They had stood by the gravesides of friends who died in storms like this. They had comforted the widows and orphaned children of friends who had gone to the deep in the midst of such a gale. The disciples knew that this night could be their last, and so they struggled to remain afloat.

The disciples were very much like most of us in that they didn't wake Jesus up when they saw the storm clouds. They didn't enlist the Savior's help when the wind first started to blow or the first few raindrops began to fall. The disciples didn't even wake Jesus up the first time the water swept over the bow of the boat. They waited until it was almost too late—until it appeared certain that they would perish—and then they cried out to Him for help.

When they did turn to Jesus, they found Him fast asleep! How could Jesus sleep through this? I imagine the disciples didn't know whether to be startled or angry that Jesus could sleep through all the commotion. We just know that they called out to awaken Him.

> The disciples went and woke him, saying, "Master, Master, we're going to drown!"
> He got up and rebuked the wind and the raging waters; the storm subsided, and all was calm (verse 24).

This is the first thing the disciples did right. They waited too long to do it, but it was the right thing to do. They cried out to Jesus for help.

And just as soon as they cried out to Jesus, what did He do? "He got up and rebuked the wind and the raging waters; the storm subsided, and all was calm" (verse 24).

The disciples cried out to Jesus, and Jesus responded. Why is this so hard for us? Why do we wait until we've tried everything else before we call out to the only One who can help? If Jesus is truly willing to calm the troubled waters of our lives, shouldn't we cry to Him first?

Bob Westenberg was taking his usual morning walk when a garbage truck pulled up beside him. He thought the driver was going to ask for directions. Instead, he pulled out a picture to show Bob—a picture of a cute little five-year-old boy. Then he said, "This is my grandson, Jeremiah. He's on a life-support system at a Phoenix hospital."

Bob thought the driver was going to ask for a contribution to the hospital bills, so he reached for his wallet. But the man wanted something more than money. He said, "I'm asking everybody I can to say a prayer for him. Would you say one for him, please?" The man realized just how helpless he was to still the troubled waters of his life, and so he responded in the only appropriate way. He cried out to God and asked others to cry out for him as well.

When the disciples called for help, Jesus stopped the storm. I've seen Him do just that. I've seen Jesus take the threat away. I've seen Him heal diseases, restore broken marriages, and turn back enemies—often immediately! Some of you who are reading this page have experienced the miracle that happens when Jesus says, "Peace, be still."

But I've also seen Jesus respond to the cry for help in a radically different way. He doesn't always make the winds stop blowing. Sometimes He chooses to allow us to remain in the midst of the storm. Instead of quieting the hurricane, He chooses to make us secure while the winds blow around us.

Jesus sometimes chooses to quiet the winds and waves inside our heart instead of quieting the strife around us. Instead of removing the trouble, Jesus reassures us that He is in control and that we can trust Him.

Gladys Aylward was a missionary to China more than sixty years ago. She was forced to flee when the Japanese invaded Yangcheng. But Gladys felt responsible for the orphans in her charge. So, with only one assistant, she led more than a hundred orphans over the mountains toward Free China.

The hardships and dangers involved in this journey were unspeakable! At every turn, Gladys risked capture or certain death for herself and the children she so desperately wanted to save. Fatigue and constant terror caused her to become depressed.

One night in particular, Gladys could not sleep. The next morning, she was filled with despair. She had absolutely no hope of reaching safety.

A thirteen-year-old girl in the group reminded her of the story of Moses and the Israelites crossing the Red Sea. After listening to the child tell the story, Gladys blurted out, "But I'm not Moses!"

The girl responded, "Of course you aren't, but Jehovah is still God!"

At that moment, hope filled Gladys's heart again. The war had not ended; the lives of the orphans were still in danger; they still had not found safety; however, Gladys's heart and mind were at peace. Jesus heard her cry and stilled the storm in her heart.

When you cry out for help, Jesus may decide to allow the cancer to run its course. He may decide to allow your business to fail or to allow you to lose your job. He may even decide to allow your wife to leave you for someone else. But all that doesn't mean that He doesn't care or that He is too weak to help. It doesn't mean that He has said "No" to your request to still the winds. It may mean that Jesus has decided that another, unseen storm is a far greater threat to you than the storm that has you so frightened just now.

We are tempted to believe that the world around us—the world we see and touch—is reality; Jesus knows that the true reality is not the seen world but the unseen, spiritual world. The real struggles in life are not the struggles against disease, poverty, and broken marriages, but the struggles against guilt, shame, unbelief, and the control Satan would exercise over our hearts and minds! Jesus' chief concern may be the storm in your heart—the storm of doubt and fear. If you will ask Him, He will quiet that storm. He will protect your boat, keeping it afloat in spite of the exterior storms. And when you know that Jesus is in charge of the storm, you can sleep in the midst of a hurricane.

During World War II, an old lady in England who had withstood the bombings with amazing courage was asked the secret of her calmness in the midst of such frightful danger. She replied, "Well, every night I say my prayers and then I remember how the parson told us God is always watching, so I go to sleep. After all, there's no need for both of us to stay awake!"

The bombings didn't end; Nazi bombers continued to fly overhead, and buzz bombs continued to hit the city almost every night. But even then, the old lady could sleep. Jesus calmed the storm in her heart, and since she trusted Him, she slept through the bombings.

Regardless of what is happening in your life, Jesus is in control. Call on Him! Ask for salvation from your storm. He may rebuke the winds or He may protect you in the midst of the storm and give you peace. You can trust Him to make that choice. Your part is simply to cry out to Him.

The disciples called on Jesus. They believed that their boat would sink and that their lives were over, so after they had tried everything else, they cried out to Jesus.

> The disciples went and woke him, saying, "Master, Master, we're going to drown!"
>
> He got up and rebuked the wind and the raging waters; the storm subsided, and all was calm. "Where is your faith?" he asked his disciples.
>
> In fear and amazement they asked one another, "Who is this? He commands even the winds and the water, and they obey him" (verses 24, 25).

"Where is your faith?" Jesus asked. That which appears so obvious to Him is a titanic struggle for us. We like to look before we leap; we want to hedge our bets. We search for security in the things we can see—the here and now.

But Jesus tells us that the things we can see and touch are unreliable. The only security is found in the One we cannot see but who is absolutely trustworthy! So He asks, "Where is your faith?"

The disciples asked that Jesus save them, and He did. He did it by speaking to the storm and having the storm obey Him.

You see, Jesus demonstrated that He is God and that as God, He is all-powerful. He has power beyond our wildest imaginations—far beyond anything we have ever seen or experienced. And when you experience such power—such overwhelming, limitless power—it makes you feel very small. It leaves you frightened.

The disciples just thought they were afraid of the storm! Real fear—gut-wrenching, palm-sweating, nerve-racking, knee-knocking fear—came when they caught just a small glimpse of the power that Jesus possessed! "In fear and amazement they asked one another, 'Who is this? He commands even the winds and the water, and they obey him' " (verse 25). Who is this? He is the only One who is trustworthy. He is God become man, and in Him all power resides!

His power is so great that to catch just a glimpse of it is enough to strike terror in your heart. But that power is the key. Because He has so much power that even the winds and the waves obey Him, we know He has the power to protect our lives today.

There is no need to fear Jesus' power because He is on your side! Jesus has promised to care for you, and He has the power to do it! He is your Redeemer, Sustainer, and Friend. Jesus may not rebuke the storm in your life, but He will go through the storm at your side. As long as Jesus is with you, you can rest easy.

Two centuries ago, a man of refinement was sentenced to spend twenty-four hours in an underground cell in an old English prison. The jailer shoved him in and slammed the prison door shut behind him. The man listened as the steps of the jailer died away in the distance. It was pitch dark in that hole deep in the bowels of the earth. The man was frightened beyond anything he had ever felt before and was certain that before long terror would drive him mad.

Then suddenly there came the sound of footsteps above, and in a quiet tone, his pastor called him by name. "John, are you there? This is your pastor."

The poor fellow gasped, "God bless you."

The pastor said, "I'll stay right here. I'll not leave until you come out."

The man's courage began to grow. His heartbeat slowed, and his breathing relaxed. He said, "As long as I know you're there, I'll be just fine."

I don't want to minimize the difficulties you may be facing today. You may be dealing with burdens so great that no one could ever imagine carrying them. Perhaps you have stood by the grave of your life partner. Maybe your lifelong dreams have been dashed. It could be that your health has been destroyed and the doctors don't know what more they can do for you. Or perhaps your spouse has rejected you and wants out. It could just be that your income is not enough to handle your outgo, and you find yourself lying awake at night trying to figure a way out when there is no way out.

You've tried everything you know, and nothing has worked. The winds are blowing, the rain is pouring, and the waves are crashing over your little boat. You realize that this could be the storm that ends all storms for you.

Maybe it's time to quit bailing and start crying for help from the only One who can save you. You can do nothing to save yourself. Your own efforts will result in your destruction, but Jesus has offered to be your refuge. He will save you.

During the Civil War, a Confederate soldier was placed on guard duty far out in the woods. The darkness of the night seemed to magnify every sound. His imagination began to run wild, and fear gripped his heart.

The man's fear was so great that it caused him to do something ill advised. He began to sing an old hymn his mother had taught him. "Jesus, Lover of my soul, let me to Thy bosom fly." Then he sang the stanza, "Other refuge have I none." As he sang, his fears diminished, and he survived the night.

After the war, this same young man was asked to sing that same song at a religious meeting. When the meeting ended, a stranger approached him and said, "I never saw you before, but I have heard that voice before." Then the stranger asked if he sang that song one night during the war.

The young man remembered that dark night in the woods and replied that he had indeed sung the song one night during the war. The stranger then told him that he and some of his men who were Union soldiers had seen him that night. They watched him from behind the trees. Just as they were ready to fire on him, they heard him begin to sing, "Jesus, Lover of my soul," and "other refuge have I none."

The stranger said, "I told my men to hold their fire. We slipped away and left you, but I shall never forget the voice I heard that night."

If you are in the midst of a storm today, allow me to encourage you. Jesus is your only refuge. He is still all-powerful, and if you will call on Him today, He will speak peace to your heart. Only He can quiet the storms of your life. Only He can give you peace.

Chapter Five

Do You Ever Feel Inferior—Broken—Disgusting?

Based on Luke 8:40–53

It was the mid to late 1980s, and the AIDS scare was at its height. Not much was known about the disease except that it was growing rapidly and seemed to spread fastest among the homosexual community. It was also known to be incurable and always lethal. People were frightened to near panic. I knew of a physician whose family quit eating out because they were afraid of contracting AIDS.

Philip Yancey writes of a young man who, during this period of panic, wrote home to tell his family that he had AIDS and was dying. He wondered if he might come home for a visit so that he might eat a Thanksgiving meal with his family one last time before he died. He received no reply, so he assumed his visit would pose no problem.

However, the visit proved to be very uncomfortable. No one hugged him, shook his hand, or touched him in any way. When it came time to eat the Thanksgiving meal, they set a small table in an adjoining room, apart from the rest of the family.

The main table was set with their finest china, but the small table where this young man ate was set with paper plates and plastic forks and knives—things that were disposable. This is where the young man with AIDS was to eat his last Thanksgiving meal. People with AIDS were the "untouchables" of society.

I have worked with people who have lost family members to AIDS. Their grief is complicated by the stigma society has attached to the disease and those who are infected with it. These families feel there is no one they can turn to for comfort or consolation.

Especially in the early days of our awareness of the disease, sufferers from the disease were made to feel as though they were the outcasts of society, the "unclean" of our day. In every age there are those who fall into this category.

In India there are distinct classes of people. I read the account from many years ago of one missionary who said that there was a class of people in India who were so low on the social scale that he had never seen one of them in the light of day. He said he had been in India for over a decade before he actually saw one of these people.

In Luke chapter 8, we find a woman who was in a class of people who were absolute outcasts from society. This woman was a social and religious outcast. She had a medical condition which, in that day, prohibited her from worshiping with other believers or even physically touching another person. And yet we find her right in the middle of the crowd pressing in on Jesus.

In the same crowd, by contrast, is Jairus. Jairus was anything but a social outcast. He was a man of high standing in the community.

It is nice to be respected in the community, and it is great to be rich and successful. But all of that is worthless when your child is so ill you are certain she will die. Jairus was panicked over the health of his only daughter.

I thank God that my daughters are healthy. I've never experienced the death of a child. But as a pastor and a chaplain, I've ministered to people who have lost children.

I remember one man, a friend of mine, who received the news that there was nothing further that the doctors could do for his eight-year-old daughter's leukemia. They had fought a long, hard battle for the girl's life, but now it was apparent that they had lost. When the reality sank in that his beloved daughter would die, this man seemed to melt before my very eyes. He buried his face in his hands and wept as he slid down the wall to the floor. I didn't know what to do, so I sat on the floor beside him and held him in my arms as we wept together. There is no panic like the panic of a parent who is about to lose a child.

Jairus felt that panic. The doctors had given up hope. His daughter was going to die. Luke tells the story. "Now when Jesus returned, a crowd welcomed him, for they were all expecting him. Then a man named Jairus, a ruler of the synagogue, came and fell at Jesus' feet, pleading with him to come to his house because his only daughter, a girl of about twelve, was dying" (Luke 8:40–42).

Jairus was a ruler of the synagogue. That means that he was a very devout Jew who was responsible for the administration of the synagogue and the ordering of public worship. Jairus had climbed to the highest position possible in the eyes of his fellow men. A man who held such a position was almost always wealthy and had the esteem of everyone in the community. To most, it probably seemed that Jairus had everything life could offer.

And yet, even this man who had everything was frightened; disease was about to rob him of his most precious possession, his daughter. Jairus couldn't imagine life without his little girl. The thought of her death was more than he could stand, and yet, he was helpless to do anything about it. What good are you as a father if you cannot help your child in her hour of greatest need?

Speaking as the father of two daughters, I can tell you that there is nothing like a "daddy's girl." Very few people can claim to be loved more than daddy's girls. When my daughters cozy up next to me, I'm completely helpless. Anything they need is theirs. There is very little that I wouldn't do for my daughters.

Jairus must have felt the same way. He loved his daughter. She was obviously a daddy's girl, and Jairus would do anything to help her.

Now, Jesus wasn't exactly high on the approval list for the leaders of Palestine. The scribes, priests, and Pharisees really didn't care for Jesus. They opposed Him at every step. For the ruler of the synagogue to approach Jesus and ask Him for such a favor meant that this man was risking his standing in the community for the chance that his little girl might be healed. He decided to take the chance.

Surprisingly, Jairus didn't approach Jesus as His peer. Instead, he fell at Jesus' feet to plead with Him as though Jesus were his superior! This was a risky thing to do, but Jairus was desperate.

Most of us who live in the United States will find it very difficult to understand the strength of the class system of those days. It was built not just on wealth and bloodlines but also on gender and on religious and political issues. The lines were rigid and not often crossed.

In addition to the isolating nature of the class system, poverty, disease, and physical and mental handicaps further separated people. These were each considered to be a curse from God. If God had punished you in such a fashion, people shunned you.

A man whom God had blessed had nothing to ask of a man whom God had cursed. Jairus was a man of wealth and religious, political, and social status. Jesus was a man of questionable birth, since His mother was pregnant before she was married to Joseph. Jesus was poor, with no real social or political status. He was an itinerate teacher whom the religious leaders of the day hated.

For Jairus to throw himself at the feet of Jesus and beg for a favor was simply unthinkable. It was social suicide! But Jairus was so desperate that he was willing to risk everything. Jairus begged Jesus to come to his house and heal his twelve-year-old daughter.

Jesus agreed and began to push through the crowd toward Jairus's house. But something happened to Jesus on the way. "As Jesus was on his way, the crowds almost crushed him. And a woman was there who had been subject to bleeding for twelve years, but no one could heal her. She came up behind him and touched the edge of his cloak, and immediately her bleeding stopped" (verses 42–44).

Remember that Jairus was the leader of his community. Jesus' journey to Jairus's house was interrupted by a woman who could be classified as being among the least in that community.

This woman's predicament is not immediately obvious to us today. First, it was bad enough just to be a woman in that day. Women could not own property, could not enter the main court of the temple in Jerusalem, could not inherit their father's wealth, and had no rights in Jewish society. While a man could divorce his wife for virtually any reason whatsoever, a woman could not divorce her husband for any reason at all! She was thought of as property.

Religious scholars of the day argued over whether or not women had souls and whether or not they could experience salvation. The prayer of thanksgiving of a devout man of that day was, "God, I thank You that You did not make me a Gentile, a sinner, or a woman!"

Now, as if this were not enough, this woman was in bad shape physically. Luke says that she had "an issue of blood," and that she had been bleeding for twelve years. This was a female problem, and it left her ceremonially unclean. That meant that she was not allowed to enter the synagogue or the temple. This woman had not been allowed to be a part of organized worship for twelve years!

But it also meant that no one was allowed to touch her for fear that they would also become ceremonially unclean and thus be prohibited from entering the temple until they had undergone a period of cleansing and a special ceremony. If she was married, it meant that she and her husband would have refrained from normal marital relations for twelve years. Her husband would not be permitted to worship in the temple or the synagogue if he had slept with his wife while she suffered from this issue of blood.

In Palestine in that day, her condition would have been grounds for her husband to divorce her. So it is possible that this woman was no longer married, and that would mean that she had no means of supporting herself other than begging.

Physically, the condition would have left her anemic, constantly in pain, and fatigued. Socially, she was alone, ostracized, and without meaningful contact—at the lowest rung of the social ladder. Everyone saw her as inferior, broken, disgusting, and pathetic. In contrast, Jairus was at the top of the social ladder. Everyone admired Jairus and believed that he was beloved of God because he enjoyed so many wonderful blessings.

While Jesus was on the way to Jairus's house, this desperate woman broke the law by pressing through the crowd and touching Jesus, something she was forbidden to do. In those days, Jews wore four white tassels on their garments. These tassels had one blue thread woven in them. This was a constant reminder that their life was devoted to God and to prayer. Most likely, the woman touched one of these tassels on Jesus' robe. And the moment she touched His robe, she was healed.

Two people from opposite ends of the social order—Jairus and this woman. Both came to Jesus to ask for help. Both came to Jesus for help—the rich and the poor, the social elite and the social outcast, the powerful and the weak, the clean and the unclean.

Ultimately, everyone is powerless and needy. We all need the power of Jesus for healing. We need Him for emotional healing; healing from sin, guilt, and shame; and healing from physical disease.

Jairus and the woman with an issue of blood teach us very important lessons. They teach us that in the final analysis, many of the things we hold so dear aren't worth very much at all! Ultimately, only a very few things really matter. Jairus discovered that the only thing that really mattered in his life was his daughter, and he would gladly forfeit everything so that she might be healed.

And the woman with an issue of blood realized that her own healing was the most important thing in her life as well. Nothing else mattered!

Even today, the only thing that matters is that we receive healing and that those we love receive healing as well. Jesus is the only source available for healing.

If you feel broken, inferior, disgusting, or otherwise in pain, there is good news for you. If you will reach out to touch Him, He will never reject you. You are not disgusting to Him. You are God's special "Daddy's boy" or "Daddy's girl," and He would do just about anything for you. Jesus loves you today and is anxious to heal you this very hour just as He healed the woman who pressed through the crowds to touch Him.

When the woman touched Jesus, He immediately recognized that something out of the ordinary had taken place.

> "Who touched me?" Jesus asked.
>
> When they all denied it, Peter said, "Master, the people are crowding and pressing against you."
>
> But Jesus said, "Someone touched me; I know that power has gone out from me."
>
> Then the woman, seeing that she could not go unnoticed, came trembling and fell at his feet. In the presence of all the people, she told why she had touched him and how she had been instantly healed. Then he said to her, "Daughter, your faith has healed you. Go in peace" (verses 45–48).

Jesus, Jairus, and the disciples were pushing their way through a throng of people in an attempt to make it to Jairus's house before his daughter died. There were hundreds, perhaps even thousands, of people who were pressing against Jesus. The disciples tried to run interference for Him as they pushed the crowd apart for Jesus to walk through. There was a lot of bumping, jostling, and even groping going on in that crowd. People were tugging at Jesus, pulling on His clothes, and grabbing for His hands as He tried to make His way to Jairus's house.

Yet in the midst of this chaos, one little sickly woman managed to get close enough to Jesus to lightly touch a prayer tassel that was attached to the hem of His garment. And when this happened, Jesus stopped and asked, "Who touched Me?" Hundreds of people were pushing, pawing, shoving, and groping, and He asked, "Who touched Me?"

But the most incredible part of this is that everyone denied having touched Him! "Not me! I didn't do it! I didn't see anyone touch You! No one touched You!"

They all lied about it! Everyone had touched Jesus, and no one admitted it.

Finally, one of the disciples spoke the obvious: "Master, everyone is pushing and crowding against You! Everyone touched You!"

But Jesus was speaking of a different kind of touch. He was speaking of a healing touch!

Isn't it comforting to know that Jesus is always able to cut through the noise of the crowd and find that one still, small voice that cries for healing? He is able to distinguish between the press of the crowd and a desperate touch in quest of healing!

Jesus wanted to demonstrate the difference between the two touches. Today, a lot of people claim to have a direct line to Jesus—they have the inside scoop, they have special knowledge, they claim to be able to speak for Jesus. They are a part of the crowd that grabs for Jesus—not in desperation as they seek to be healed, but in a manner that seeks to control or to use the power and authority of Jesus to control others. But they do not control Jesus.

By contrast, when the lowest of the low, the weakest of the weak, desperately reaches out for a healing touch, Jesus pays attention. He stops and makes that one person His top priority!

This is a truly amazing thing about Jesus. Very often, religionists have less access to Jesus than does the worst sinner who simply confesses his need.

The religious leaders in Jesus' day were legalists. They thought of religion as a list of "do's" and "don't's" rather than as a relationship with the living God. They thought they could appease God through avoiding negative behavior and embracing positive behavior. But such an approach to religion is always deadly.

It doesn't take very long to realize that this approach to religion leaves the practitioner empty. You never feel "good enough." There never comes a time when you have done enough to feel the acceptance of the Father. So the tendency is to compare yourself with others and say, "I may not be perfect, but at least I'm better than Joe!"

Legalists are careful to set the standard for God's acceptance at a mark just below where they think they stand. By so doing, they grasp for control of Jesus. They attempt to reshape Jesus in their own image. Therefore, legalism is blind to its need. A legalist can never afford to take a long, hard look at himself because to do so would require admitting that all the effort to be "good enough" has been a futile waste of time. So legalism never sees its need.

Such religion is best described in the message to the church of Laodicea. Jesus says to that church, " 'You say, "I am rich; I have acquired wealth and do not need a thing." But you do not realize that you are wretched, pitiful, poor, blind and naked' " (Revelation 3:17).

Those who grab for Jesus in an effort to control Him will never do so. They have no access to Him. But anyone who recognizes and confesses his inadequacies will never be turned away. Access to Jesus is provided only when we recognize that our sinfulness leaves us in desperate need of spiritual healing. The religious leaders of Jesus' day didn't think of themselves as sinners. Therefore, they never benefited from His healing touch.

When the woman with an issue of blood came to Jesus, she did so in desperation. She knew she could not help herself, and she knew she had nothing to offer to the One she believed could heal her. That's why she was healed when she touched Jesus.

Jesus said, "Someone touched Me; I know that power has gone out from Me." When even the outcasts of society admit their need and humbly reach out to Jesus for healing, that simple touch unleashes the power of Heaven! The power of God is at the disposal of any poor wretch who asks for it!

Society, family, friends, or even the church may have made you feel unworthy, broken, rejected, and even disgusting, but the God of heaven loves you so much that His great heart is moved by your need. He will respond to your plea for help and heal you. He loves you, accepts you, and forgives you today!

Truthfully, you may not have some dread disease that separates you from society, and you may not carry a social stigma that leaves you unacceptable to people around you, but you may still feel inferior and rejected.

One man told me of a hidden sin in his life that left him with a load of guilt and shame. No one knew about the sin but him, and yet the guilt made him feel inferior to everyone.

You need not be able to point to a particular, hidden sin in your life to feel a need of healing. You may feel a lot more like Jairus than the woman with an issue of blood. You don't have to be the refuse of society to need or receive the healing touch of Jesus.

Jesus interrupted His day in order to go to Jairus's house and heal his daughter. And even though He was interrupted, eventually, He did heal the girl. Jairus's daughter died before Jesus reached the house, but He raised her from the dead and made her whole.

The key was that both Jairus and the woman came humbly before Jesus and acknowledged their need.

These two people from very different social strata admitted that they were powerless to help themselves and asked for Jesus' intervention in their lives. Jesus always responds to such a plea for help, regardless of your position in life.

As Jesus walked that day, He knew that someone had touched Him in faith, and now He wanted to acknowledge—even honor—the touch of this rejected woman. Jesus asked, "Who touched Me?"

The disciples said, "Lord, everyone touched You! This whole crowd has been pushing and shoving against You and grabbing for You!"

But Jesus said, "No, not that kind of touch. Someone touched Me in faith and was healed."

The woman, seeing that Jesus wasn't going to allow her to slip quietly away, finally came forward and admitted that she had touched Him and that she had been healed. Observe how Jesus responds to this woman. See how Jesus treats those who feel broken, inferior, guilty, shame-ridden, and rejected! Notice what He calls the woman whom everyone else had rejected. He calls her "daughter"! Jesus called this broken outcast of society "daughter." "Daughter, your faith has healed you. Go in peace."

Jesus was on His way to heal a "daddy's girl," but He wanted everyone to know that the woman whom they had rejected was also a "daddy's girl"! God felt the same way about this woman as Jairus felt about his twelve-year-old daughter. She was God's little girl, the apple of His eye, and God was just as anxious to help both of His little girls as Jairus was to help his daughter.

The woman whom Jesus healed that day received more than just physical healing. She received healing for heart and soul.

Jesus called her "daughter." Such tender words for someone who hadn't felt the touch of human kindness for twelve years! Such loving acceptance for someone who had been rejected for over a decade! This is how Jesus treats the broken. This is how Jesus deals with the rejected.

Dear wounded soul, this is how Jesus treats you today! He will not turn you away. He will not reject you. He does not see you as others see you. He sees you as His own precious daughter, His own precious son. You do not need to clean up your act before you come to Jesus any more than this woman needed to heal herself before she touched the hem of His garment. He wants you exactly as you are right now! He longs to take the brokenness of your life and heal you.

Others may be appalled at your sin. They may look at you and wonder how anyone could love or accept you, much less a holy God! But this story tells us that regardless of your sin, regardless of your feelings of brokenness, and regardless of how often you have been rejected by others, God is anxious to receive you today, to forgive you, to heal you, and to accept you as His own.

Take note of His love! Be amazed by His grace—grace that forgives the worst of sinners—and thrill as Jesus satisfies the desire of your heart.

Taysi Abu Saada, a PLO member also known as Tass, was a committed terrorist, determined to kill as many Jews as possible. Tass was trained as a

Fatah sniper. It was his duty to kill Jews, and he taught children that it was their duty to kill Jews. Tass's heart was filled with hatred for all Jews.

Moran Rosenblit was a soldier in the Israeli army. Moran grew to hate the PLO after a suicide bomber killed seven of his friends. He wanted to wipe them off the face of the earth!

Tass left the Middle East and moved to Kansas City, where a co-worker, named Charlie, introduced Tass to Jesus. As Tass saw Jesus' life of perfect love, it opened his eyes to the ugliness of his own life. Jesus taught children to love, while Tass had taught children to hate and to kill. Jesus came to save life, while Tass had been a sniper who had taken life. The contrast could not have been clearer. Tass saw himself for what he was—a sinner, who had no possibility of making things right—in his own strength.

But Jesus accepted Tass as he was. He received him as His own, and that realization changed his life completely. Where there had been hatred, there was now only love.

At the same time this was happening to Tass, Moran was suffering deeply from grief over the loss of his friends to the hateful act of the suicide bomber. His anger and resentment would not even allow him to attend the funerals for his friends!

Moran's hatred grew daily and was not helped by the collision of two Israeli helicopters that left eighty-six soldiers dead. Although none were Moran's friends, their deaths added to his grief and hatred.

A Swedish girlfriend saw Moran's pain and encouraged him to leave Israel. He first went to England and then on to California. There he roomed with a Christian family. Through their witness and the help of friends, Moran learned of Jesus.

For the first time in his life, Moran realized just how disgusting prejudice and hatred really are. He saw his own ugly prejudice contrasted with Jesus' perfect love and acceptance. But as he saw this, he also saw that Jesus had not rejected him for his prejudice but was actually willing to accept and forgive him. Moran's heart melted. He accepted Jesus as his Messiah and was baptized.

Months after Moran's conversion, a friend invited him to a conference for Arab and Jewish believers. While at the conference, Moran reluctantly accepted an invitation to share his testimony at another conference. He anguished over what to say, but finally gave an honest, detailed account of his life of hatred, resentment, and grief before accepting Jesus as his Savior.

After Moran finished speaking, a Palestinian man approached him and said, "I was a Fatah fighter." The man was Tass. Tass looked Moran in the eyes and added, "I love you."

Later, Moran said, "I can't explain what it did to my heart when he said that."

Tass asked Moran to forgive him and his people for the death of his friends who were killed by the suicide bomber. Moran forgave Tass and his people but also sought forgiveness for his anger and hatred for Tass's people. Since that conference in March 2001, Moran and Tass have become great friends. They speak to one another daily. Tass says, "Jesus touched my heart. It goes to show the world there is hope in Jesus." Moran adds, "Do you want a picture of the solution for the Middle East? If God changed my heart and Tass's heart, He can change anyone's heart."

Jesus forgave Tass and Moran. Many would look at these two men and see something very disgusting. After all, they were men whose lives had been defined by hatred, prejudice, and murder. But Jesus forgave these two angry men. Jesus loved, accepted, and changed Tass and Moran.

This is how God treats those who feel inferior, broken, and disgusting. It is how God has promised to treat you.

Don't be afraid to confess your desperate need of Him. Reach out and touch the hem of His garment. He will not turn you away! You are His beloved child!

Chapter Six

Would You Like to Live Forever?

Based on Luke 10:25–37

I have not met many people who don't want to go to heaven. I've met people who don't believe there is such a thing as heaven, but even then, most of them will say that if there should happen to be such a thing as heaven, they'd like to go.

Most of the people I talk to want to go to heaven, even though they often can't tell you a lot about what heaven is like. They're not really sure what people do in heaven, but they know that people in heaven live forever, and that sounds pretty good to them. People want to live forever in a place that is perfect.

We don't want much; we just want everything—eternal life with perpetual happiness!

The desire for heaven and eternal life is an old one. It has been around for quite a while.

Genesis tells us that the serpent promised that Eve could do whatever she wanted—and still live forever. Eve was beguiled by the offer and gave in to temptation.

According to legend, King Arthur and his Knights of the Round Table sought the Holy Grail. It was not just the cup from the Last Supper; it was the cup into which the very blood of Jesus was shed. Legend had it that anyone who could find the cup and drink its contents would never die.

Explorer Ponce de León searched Florida for the Fountain of Youth—a fountain whose waters would bestow upon you the blessings of eternal youth. Today, as a nation, we spend billions on health care, diets, medications, and exercise equipment and programs, as well as cosmetic surgery, in an attempt to stave off the ravages of old age or cheat the grave.

Biotechnologists in Iceland report they have advanced the search for the secret to eternal life by locating the gene responsible for healthy old age. The gene has been named the "Methuselah gene," after the Old Testament figure who lived for 969 years.

The researchers discovered that those who live longer appeared to have inherited a single gene that protects them against old age—giving them ten to fifteen more years of life than the average. Scientists now say it may be possible to make drugs to replicate the action of this specific aging gene and provide longer life for everyone.

Ultimately, however, all our efforts to live forever will fall short of that mark. We may add ten or fifteen years to the life span, but eventually, death will come to all. When death draws near, even avowed atheists often begin to look to God for the hope that they might live again.

I spent a number of years working as a hospice chaplain and a hospital chaplain. It was my job to offer a visit to every patient, even those whose religious preference was listed as "atheist." I never found an atheist whose condition was listed as terminal refuse a visit from the chaplain. Further, I never saw an avowed atheist who entered into an honest conversation regarding the possibility that God exists die as an atheist. Somehow, they put aside their skepticism in order to believe in God and the possibility of eternal life.

Scripture assures us that it is possible to live forever. A story in the book of Luke explores this very issue. Luke tells us, "On one occasion an expert in the law stood up to test Jesus. 'Teacher,' he asked, 'what must I do to inherit eternal life?' " (Luke 10:25).

The man who asked Jesus about eternal life is referred to as "an expert in the law." Religious leaders of the day felt that the scriptural law was God's best word to the world. They believed that in the law they could find answers to every question. The most rewarding pursuit in life was a study of God's law.

But notice that the man asked, "What must I *do* to inherit eternal life?" His emphasis was on performance or personal activity.

Religious leaders of that day believed that obedience to the law was the key to winning eternal life. They believed that if the whole of Israel would perfectly obey the law for even one day, the Messiah would come. The Messiah, in their minds, was the one who would throw off the yoke of Roman oppression and restore Israel to the status of a great nation. But everything depended upon perfect obedience to the law.

Perhaps this expert in the law had something like this in mind when he asked his question of Jesus. The man seemed to be asking a behavioral question, but Jesus wanted to move away from behavior toward relationship, so He answered the man's question with another question—a leading question: " 'What is written in the law?' he replied. 'How do you read it?' " (verse 26).

When Jesus asked, "How do you read it?" He was referring to something the man could read right then and there. The devout, in those days, wore little leather boxes around their wrists called phylacteries. These phylacteries contained certain passages of Scripture and were to be a constant reminder of the person's obligation to God. The passages contained in the phylacteries were Exodus 13:1–10; Deuteronomy 6:4–9; and Deuteronomy 11:13–20. Jesus seemed to be saying, "Open up your phylactery and read to Me what the law says regarding your question."

The man read to Jesus the passage from Deuteronomy 6:4 and Deuteronomy 11:13: "He answered: ' "Love the Lord your God with all your heart and with all your soul and with all your strength and with all your mind;" and, "Love your neighbor as yourself" ' " (verse 27). The passages in Deuteronomy tell us to love God wholeheartedly. To this, the scribes of the day added Leviticus 19:18, which commands us to love our neighbors as ourselves. However, this man was seeking a new commandment—something more he could do to be assured he was doing that which was necessary to have eternal life.

Jesus didn't add a new commandment. He didn't add a new behavior. Instead, He referred the man back to the commands he wore on his wrists. He told the man to love God and love his neighbor. Jesus gave a relational answer to a behavioral question.

The religious leaders of that day had a very narrow definition of the word *neighbor.* They would not include in that term anyone who was not of the same gender, race, or religion as they were. In fact, some religious leaders declared that if you helped a Gentile woman at the time of childbirth, you were breaking the law, because you were helping to bring another Gentile into the world!

Think about that! To them, it became an act of devotion to allow a baby to die, as long as the baby was of a different race than their own!

How is it that so many people have taken religion and used it to justify the most heinous acts? Prejudice, hatred, and even war have all been justified by some religious tenet.

Christians fought the Crusades in order to free the Holy Land of pagans. In Ireland, Catholics and Protestants fight each other in the name of Christianity. In the Middle East, Jews and Palestinians do the same in the name of religion. Some radical Muslims wage "holy war" against "infidels," which includes anyone who does not agree with them. To them, taking innocent life is not just permissible, but is even desirable, as long as it helps them accomplish their "holy" goals.

How does this happen? Clearly, such hatreds and divisions do not fit with religious teachings. Jesus never justified such unholy practices in the name of religion.

Whenever religion justifies, or even encourages, the taking of innocent life in order to fulfill its goals, you can be sure that such a religion is not from God.

The religious leaders in Jesus' day had sought to justify all sorts of prejudice through their religion. They obviously did not think of anyone who was not of their race as their neighbor. In fact, many of these same leaders declared that God had created Gentiles to fuel the fires of hell!

Jesus was aware of this type of prejudicial, myopic thinking. He wanted to broaden the thinking of this expert in the law, but first, He attempted to find some common ground with the man.

Remember, the man had quoted the scriptural requirement that we love God with all our heart, soul, strength, and mind, and that we love our neighbor as ourselves. Jesus confirmed that he had answered well. " 'You have answered correctly,' Jesus replied. 'Do this and you will live' " (verse 28).

Some have wondered about Jesus' answer. He seems to be supporting the idea that one could earn or deserve salvation. Nothing could be further from the truth. While it was obvious that the expert in the law was thinking of these things from a purely behavioral viewpoint, Jesus had a much broader, more relational viewpoint in mind.

But the man wanted everyone to know that he had done these things. He wanted to justify himself, so he asked another question, "And who is my neighbor?"

How would you answer that question? Who is your neighbor? Is it that group of people you know and love? Is your family the only group that qualifies as your neighbor? Do you limit the definition of neighbor to people of your religious group, race, nationality, or socioeconomic class?

George Eldon Ladd wrote: "Jesus redefines the meaning of love for neighbor; it means love for any man in need."

Haddon Robinson writes that when his son, Tory, was just a small boy, they were coming home from church when Haddon asked Tory what he had learned that morning. Tory told him they had heard the story of the Good Samaritan. He proceeded to give a blow-by-blow description of what had taken place.

When he was all through, Haddon said, "Son, what was the spiritual lesson of the story?"

Tory thought for a minute and said, "That story teaches that whenever I'm in trouble, you've got to help me."

From the viewpoint of the man on the side of the road, that's about as good a definition of what it means to be a neighbor as you're going to find. Your neighbor is anyone who is in need, regardless of age, gender, race, or creed.

The Bible tells us that those who find eternal life will be those who demonstrate genuine love for God and for anyone who is in need. It begins with God's love for us. When we understand just how much God loves us, it stirs our hearts with love for Him. As that love grows, and we grow in deeper relationship with God, God places a love for other people in our hearts—a love even for our enemies.

Georgia Harkness wrote, "Christian love links love of God and love of neighbor in a twofold Great Commandment from which neither element can be dropped, so sin against neighbor through lack of human love is sin against God."

Jesus declares that God cares how you treat people—all people! All men are your neighbors, and all men deserve to be treated with love. If we are to live forever, this is how we will live.

Jesus said that love is the key. We are to love God, and we are to love our neighbor.

The expert in the law asked a question typical of religious leaders of his day. They felt their job was, in part, to define terms so that they might prescribe behavior. In their religious system, behavior was the key to winning eternal life. So the expert in the law asked for a definition of the word *neighbor.*

Jesus answered his question by telling a story.

In reply Jesus said: "A man was going down from Jerusalem to Jericho, when he fell into the hands of robbers. They stripped him of his clothes, beat him and went away, leaving him half dead. A priest happened to be going down the same road, and when he saw the man, he passed by on the other side. So too, a Levite, when he came to the place and saw him, passed by on the other side. But a Samaritan, as he traveled, came where the man was; and when he saw him, he took pity on him. He went to him and bandaged his wounds, pouring on oil and wine. Then he put the man on his own donkey, took him to an inn and took care of him. The next day he took out two silver coins and gave them to the innkeeper. 'Look after him,' he said, 'and when I return, I will reimburse you for any extra expense you may have.'

"Which of these three do you think was a neighbor to the man who fell into the hands of robbers?"

The expert in the law replied, "The one who had mercy on him."

Jesus told him, "Go and do likewise" (verses 30–37).

This story had an edge to it, because the Jews had absolutely no dealings with Samaritans. They looked down on these people of mixed race and confused religious ideas. "Samaritan" was a term used to refer either to someone from Samaria or to someone who was a heretic and a breaker of the ceremonial law. The fact that Jesus made a Samaritan the hero of His story and the religious leadership of Israel the goat was not lost on His listeners.

The story takes place on the road from Jerusalem to Jericho. This road was notorious for the highwaymen who preyed on defenseless travelers. Jerusalem is 2,300 feet above sea level. Jericho is near the Dead Sea and is 1,300 feet below sea level. The distance between the two cities is less than twenty miles, so in less in twenty miles this road dropped 3,600 feet.

It was a narrow, winding road that wove between rocky crags that made excellent hiding places for the thieves who infested the area. It was called "The Red Way" or "Blood Way" because of all the people who were ambushed there.

William Barclay tells us that as recently as the early 1930s a thief named Abu Jildah was famous for stopping cars, robbing the passengers, and escaping before the police could arrive. This is the road the man was traveling on in Jesus' story when robbers accosted him.

Now, what does all this background information tell you about the man who was traveling from Jerusalem to Jericho? Since this road was notorious for being infested with thieves, why would a man attempt such a trip alone? Doesn't this tell you that the man was foolish? Doesn't it tell you that, at least in part, this man brought misfortune upon himself?

The priest and the Levite who refused to help the man may have felt this way. I've heard people question the wisdom of helping people who make bad decisions. After all, if we help them, they'll just go out and do it again. Helping such people only enables them to continue to live foolishly. Yet, Jesus is describing a situation where a man helped someone who had experienced disaster because of his own foolish choice. That didn't stop the Samaritan from helping.

Those who oppose helping people who make bad decisions are actually putting themselves at risk. The suggestion is that people should not make repeated wrong choices. People should be able to make wise choices, and if they fail to make wise choices, they should not complain when they experience the consequences of their choices and no one offers to help.

If we apply that same principle to God's dealings with us, we run into a lot of trouble. The vast majority of our sins result from foolish choices—even repeated foolish choices. If God treated us the way we propose to treat others, then we would have absolutely no chance for salvation. God would simply say, "If I forgive you and help you, you'll just go out and do it again! You made the decision, and now you should be willing to shoulder the pain of being lost!"

But the story of the Good Samaritan reveals to us not just how we are to treat those who are in need because of their foolish choices but also how God relates to us when we choose foolishly.

This is a story of grace, and grace assures us that God is willing to rescue us even when we are repeatedly foolish!

The point of the story is that anyone in need is my neighbor. God tells us that it is because our need is so great that He sees us as His neighbors. That means that even when we are in trouble because of our own foolish choices, God still loves us and is willing to forgive us and help us! God extends His saving grace to His foolish neighbors—and you and I are the foolish neighbors!

Jesus was saying that the way to heaven begins with accepting the fact that God loves us even when we are foolish, bad, and downright disgusting, and in response to such love we are to love God right back. That love will eventually result in our loving others the same way God loves us. This type of grace-filled relationship with God is the way to live forever!

Please understand, we are not saved because we love our neighbor. Loving our neighbor is more the natural result of having been saved by the grace of God and experiencing His love. Salvation comes first; love for neighbor follows salvation.

Jesus made this very clear when He explained the way of salvation. John quotes Jesus in chapter 5 of his Gospel: " 'I tell you the truth, whoever hears my word and believes him who sent me has eternal life and will not be condemned; he has crossed over from death to life' " (John

5:24). Salvation comes through believing in Jesus. It comes through a saving relationship with Christ. Salvation is not about our works, it is about believing in Jesus.

The expert in the law wanted to know which rules to keep so that he might earn eternal life. Jesus pointed him away from behavior and toward relationship. The apostle Paul understood this and emphasized it in his letter to the church at Ephesus: "For it is by grace you have been saved, through faith—and this not from yourselves, it is the gift of God—not by works, so that no one can boast" (Ephesians 2:8, 9).

Grace can be defined as "unmerited favor." In other words, when you receive something good that you don't deserve, you have received grace. If you will have faith in Jesus, you will receive the gift of His grace; you will receive life eternal.

How do we do this? What is the procedure for receiving the grace of God? Let's look at what Paul says in his letter to the church in Rome. "That if you confess with your mouth, 'Jesus is Lord,' and believe in your heart that God raised him from the dead, you will be saved. For it is with your heart that you believe and are justified, and it is with your mouth that you confess and are saved. As the Scripture says, 'Anyone who trusts in him will never be put to shame' " (Romans 10:9–11).

Paul says that we are to "confess" verbally that "Jesus is Lord." This means that we openly and freely admit that Jesus is more than just a good man or a great teacher, that He is, in fact, God. Jesus is the Lord of the universe, and Jesus is Lord of our life.

Paul also says that we are to "believe" something. But this is not just head knowledge. We are to believe it in our hearts. This is to be an experiential, relational belief, and the thing that we are to believe in this experiential, relational manner is that God raised Jesus from the grave. If we do this, we will be saved. This means that God will give us life without end!

All of this is about a relationship. We know that because of verse 11. Paul says, "Anyone who trusts in him will never be put to shame."

I cannot trust someone I don't know personally. I trust my wife. I've known her intimately as my wife for twenty-nine years. Twenty-nine years of marriage have taught me that Gayle is trustworthy.

If I am to trust in Jesus, I must know Him. I must have a relationship with Him. That is what Jesus is saying in this story.

Remember, all of this started with the man's question, "What must I do to inherit eternal life?" Jesus answered his question by talking about relationships of love—saving relationships. And when we know, love, and trust Jesus, He makes it possible for us to love anyone who is in need. As Erwin Lutzer said, "God loved the world. Go thou and do likewise."

I would like to share a story of a man who did just that. Maximilian Kolbe was a Catholic priest in Poland whom the Nazis arrested in February 1941 and sent to Auschwitz. Life expectancy there for a priest was about a month.

He soon faced imminent death after the guards beat him and left him for dead. Fellow prisoners nursed him to survival, and he was transferred to Barracks 14.

In July, a prisoner escaped from Kolbe's barracks, so Commandant Fritsch declared that ten prisoners would die in the starvation bunker for the one who escaped. The guards called out ten names, and one of the ten cried out, "My poor wife! My poor children! What will they do?"

Maximilian Kolbe pleaded with the commandant, "I would like to die in place of one of the men you condemned." Never had there been such a request! Nonetheless, he was permitted to die for the man he chose—prisoner 5659, the one who cried out for his wife and family.

Maximilian was then stripped of his clothes and marched with the other nine to their grave, the basement of Barracks 14. It was dark and hot. There was no food or water because they were there to die.

As days passed by, the usual screams were not heard. To the contrary, faint sounds of singing arose from the basement.

By August 14, all but four prisoners were dead. The living skeleton of Kolbe was one who was still alive. He was propped against the wall with a ghost of a smile on his lips. Like the other three, he was given a lethal injection, and death relieved his pain.

Maximilian Kolbe died with the victory he had prayed for earlier: "Christ's cross has triumphed over its enemies in every age. I believe, in the end, even in these darkest days in Poland, the cross will triumph over the swastika. I pray I can be faithful to that end."

The Cross makes it possible for one to give his life for his neighbor. The Cross makes it possible for you to live forever.

Come to Jesus today. Receive His love and accept His gift of life everlasting today. Then allow the gift of God's love to change your life. Allow it to help you love your neighbors, even the neighbors who are difficult to love. God so loved the world—now go and do likewise!

Chapter Seven

How Do You Get to Know a God You Cannot See?

Based on Luke 11

A young soldier who was fighting in Italy during World War II jumped into a foxhole just ahead of a shower of bullets. He immediately tried to deepen the hole for more protection and was frantically scraping away the dirt with his hands. As he dug, he unearthed something metal and brought up a silver crucifix left by a former resident of the foxhole.

A moment later another figure landed beside him as the shells screamed overhead. When the soldier got a chance to look, he saw that his new companion was an army chaplain.

Holding out the crucifix, the soldier gasped, "Am I glad to see you! How do you work this thing?"

In moments of crisis we may feel very much like this soldier, but prayer is certainly not relegated to emergencies. Prayer is to be a part of our daily lives. Martin Luther said, "As it is the business of tailors to make clothes and of cobblers to mend shoes, so it is the business of Christians to pray."

Why is it the business of Christians to pray? What is the purpose of prayer, and how are we to pray? Jesus speaks to these issues in chapter 11 of Luke's Gospel: "One day Jesus was praying in a certain place. When he finished, one of his disciples said to him, 'Lord, teach us to pray, just as John taught his disciples' " (verse 1).

It is interesting to me to notice that the disciples never asked Jesus to teach them how to preach. Jesus spent a great deal of time teaching and preaching. His words moved people to action and had a great effect on the masses. The religious leaders of the day were upset at the words of Jesus; His words caused them great alarm. Yet the disciples never asked Jesus to teach them to preach. They did ask Him, however, to teach them to pray.

Have you ever wondered why? I believe the disciples realized that the power Jesus demonstrated in His words and deeds came from His prayer life.

Repeatedly, the Scriptures tell us that Jesus arose early in the morning and went out to a deserted place to pray. Often the disciples would awake and realize that Jesus was gone. They would search for Him and find Him alone and in prayer.

Jesus seemed to be addicted to prayer. He spent countless hours speaking to His Father in prayer. Prayer was the source of power for His life.

Through the centuries, others have discovered this same source of power for life and for ministry. That great figure of the Reformation Martin Luther was definitely a man of prayer. This man of God endured many hardships, persecutions, and challenges in his life and ministry. His days and nights were filled with urgent work, and yet Luther wrote, "I am so busy now that if I did not spend two or three hours each day in prayer, I would not get through the day."

In the midst of the Civil War, President Abraham Lincoln wrote, "I have been driven many times to my knees by the overwhelming conviction that I had nowhere else to go. My own wisdom, and that of all about me, seemed insufficient for the day."

During the nineteenth century, Charles Haddon Spurgeon was known as "The Prince of Preachers." His sermons had a great effect on his listeners. This great man of God said, "All the Christian virtues are locked up in the word *prayer.*"

During the nineteenth and early twentieth century, there was no greater evangelist than D. L. Moody. This humble, yet powerful, preacher was loved and respected as a true Christian man. Moody wrote: "I'd rather be able to pray than be a great preacher; Jesus Christ never taught His disciples how to preach, but only how to pray."

The disciples watched Jesus' life and realized that the time spent in prayer was the secret of His power, and so they wanted Jesus to teach them how to pray. Jesus responded to this request with a prayer we know as the Lord's Prayer. Luke gives us an abbreviated version of this prayer, but Matthew, while relating the same experience, gives a longer version:

> This, then, is how you should pray:
> "Our Father in heaven,
> hallowed be your name,
> your kingdom come,
> your will be done
>   on earth as it is in heaven.
> Give us today our daily bread.
> Forgive us our debts,
>   as we also have forgiven our debtors.
> And lead us not into temptation,
> but deliver us from the evil one" (Matthew 6:9).

Notice that the closing we are all familiar with is not included either in Luke or in Matthew in the New International Version. While you do find it in the King James Version, most scholars believe that the closing was not a part of the original prayer but was added by someone who was copying the manuscript at a much later time. Even though it may not be in the original text, the closing certainly does not take away from the prayer but may actually add value to it—"For yours is the kingdom, the power, and the glory for ever. Amen."

Let's take a look at this prayer as we learn something of how we ought to pray.

First, the prayer begins by calling God "Father." This is a very personal name and represented a radical departure from the Old Testament pattern of addressing God.

Jesus could have told us to refer to God as many things—Majesty, King, Lord, or the Hebrew Yahweh. However, He chose to have us call Him Father.

Jesus spoke Aramaic and used the Aramaic word *Abba,* which is similar to our word "Daddy." The disciples must have gasped to hear Jesus refer to God by such an intimate, personal term. It was something unheard of in Old Testament literature! Jesus was demonstrating that the Father is accessible to us, just as a loving earthly father is anxious to hear from and answer his children.

Jesus further identified the Father as being in heaven. Heaven is the name given to the place where God dwells. God is spirit and cannot be contained in any one place, but He is spoken of here as being in heaven in order to teach us of God's transcendence.

God is so great, so big, and so different from anything we know that He cannot be confined to a locality. He is above all things and separate from all things—He is altogether holy. Yet, as our Father, He has chosen to be accessible to us.

The story is told of a Union soldier who, in the midst of the Civil War, desired an audience with President Lincoln. His brothers had been killed, leaving him as the sole surviving son of his widowed mother. She had written her last son to tell him that if he didn't come home to harvest the crops, they would rot in the fields, and she would surely lose the farm.

The only person who could grant permission for this soldier to take a leave of absence was the president; however, day after day the soldier had been turned away, unable to have an audience with the president.

Time was running out. His division was soon to be redeployed. The soldier made one final attempt to see his commander in chief but was once again turned away. Dejected, he slowly walked away from the White House, resigned to the fact that the family farm was lost.

As he was walking, he was so deep in grief that he nearly tripped over a small boy who was playing with a ball on the White House lawn. The boy asked the soldier to play catch with him. This was the last thing the soldier wanted to do, but the boy was so insistent that the soldier agreed. Soon the ball was flying back and forth between the two of them.

After a while, the boy asked the soldier why he was at the White House. The soldier told the boy of the family emergency and then added, "But the president is too busy to see me. I can't get in to see him."

With that, the boy grabbed the soldier's hand and said, "Follow me." He marched the soldier up the White House steps, past the guards at the front door, through the halls, and right to the door of the Oval Office!

Upon seeing the boy, the soldiers who stood guard stepped aside. The boy opened the door, and before he realized it, the soldier stood before the president of the United States!

President Lincoln was working at his desk as they entered. He looked up, saw the boy, and said, "Hello, Tad! Who is your friend?"

Tad Lincoln introduced the soldier and explained his plight. And, you guessed it, President Lincoln granted the soldier a leave of absence so that he might harvest the crops and save the family farm.

The soldier had been unable to gain access to the president, but the president's son always had access. Just so, as sons and daughters of the Most High God, we also have access to our heavenly Daddy!

But, even though we are invited to refer to God by a very intimate name, we are not to forget that He is holy. In fact, we are to hallow His very name. This is the first petition of the Lord's Prayer, and it reminds us that this is God's first priority—that His name be hallowed.

God's name is an expression of Himself. We hallow His name as a means of acknowledging that He alone is God.

Christian author R. C. Sproul tells us that the Old Testament was written primarily in Hebrew. In that language there are no adjectives. In place of adjectives, Hebrew uses repetition. If someone fell into a pit, that was one thing. But if the pit was a very large pit, the Hebrew writers simply repeated the word *pit,* saying that the person fell into a "pit pit." This conveyed the idea that this pit was very large.

In describing God's character, one characteristic of God is taken beyond mere repetition all the way to the third degree. Only God's holiness is taken to that level.

Isaiah 6 tells of an experience of Isaiah, while in vision, being taken into the very throne room of God. Isaiah saw smoke and angels and God "high and lifted up" on His throne. The angels sang a song of God's character. The song they sang was "Holy, holy, holy." They did not repeat the word *holy* three times because it fit the music. They repeated it three times because the holiness of God is far beyond anything we could ever imagine.

Nowhere is God declared to be "love, love, love," or "mercy, mercy, mercy," or "justice, justice, justice." But He is declared to be "holy, holy, holy."

When we pray "hallowed be your name," we are to take note of the holiness of God. God is completely holy. He is totally without sin. Nothing unholy can survive His presence. God's name is hallowed because He is completely holy.

The next verse in the prayer is "your kingdom come, your will be done on earth as it is in heaven." This is a prayer for the return of Christ and the establishment of His kingdom on earth. This was the major thrust of Christ's preaching while here on earth.

It is also a prayer that Christ's kingdom be established here and now—not just at the end of time, but now. It is a prayer that God's will be accomplished on the face of the earth.

More importantly, it is a prayer that His will be accomplished in our lives today. His will is to be done in me; He is to be the Lord of my life. I am to be obedient to His commands and receptive of His will.

There is a sense in which these first three petitions are all the same concept, repeated in three different ways for emphasis. In the Hebrew language, when a thing was thought to be of the greatest importance or was to be expressed as an absolute superlative, it was repeated three times. Obedience that honors God's name, establishes His kingdom on earth, and fulfills His will is of primary importance to God.

Next, the prayer reads, "Give us this day our daily bread." This reminds us that we do not provide for our own needs. God makes provision for us. All that we have belongs to God. All that we have we receive from God. We are totally dependent upon our holy, sovereign God even for the necessities of daily living.

The prayer continues, "Forgive us our debts, as we also have forgiven our debtors."

We are promised that forgiveness from sin is immediate upon our confession. In 1 John 1:9 we read, "If we confess our sins, he is faithful and just and will forgive us our sins and purify us from all unrighteousness."

Our forgiveness is certain! Only one thing can cause us to lose the forgiveness we so freely receive from God, and that is our refusal to forgive others. Jesus tells us that God will judge us in the same manner as we judge other people. God requires that we give to others the same grace we have received.

The next phrase is "And lead us not into temptation, but deliver us from the evil one." This petition follows the Old Testament form of parallelism, which says the same thing in two different ways. This is a prayer that God will protect us from the attacks of Satan. It is a prayer to keep us from giving in to temptation. On our own, we are powerless to avoid doing evil. God alone can deliver us.

The closing petition "For yours is the kingdom, the power, and the glory for ever. Amen," while not in the oldest manuscripts, is a fitting close to the prayer. It summarizes the prayer's opening and reminds us of the One who hears our prayers.

This is the pattern for prayer that Jesus gave His disciples. It is more than just an effective pattern for prayer. It teaches us something about God. It tells us that our holy, sovereign God loves us and longs to give us good gifts, if we will but ask.

Above all, this prayer teaches us that the greatest gift God has to offer is the gift of Himself. More than anything else, prayer introduces us to the One who loves us and who alone can bring blessings to our lives.

In Luke 11, after Jesus gave the disciples their beginner's lesson in prayer, He helped them take the next step in understanding prayer. He did this, once again, by telling them a story and using an illustration:

> Then he said to them, "Suppose one of you has a friend, and he goes to him at midnight and says, 'Friend, lend me three loaves of bread, because a friend of mine on a journey has come to me, and I have nothing to set before him.'
>
> "Then the one inside answers, 'Don't bother me. The door is already locked, and my children are with me in bed. I can't get up and give you anything.' I tell you, though he will not get up and give him the bread because he is his friend, yet because of the man's boldness he will get up and give him as much as he needs.
>
> "So I say to you: Ask and it will be given to you; seek and you will find; knock and the door will be opened to you. For everyone

who asks receives; he who seeks finds; and to him who knocks, the door will be opened" (verses 5–10).

Here, Jesus taught the disciples a lesson about perseverance in prayer more by means of contrast than example.

The story is of a friend who hears the request of his neighbor, has the ability to meet the request, but because he does not want to be bothered, refuses to meet the need. This doesn't sound like a great friend! But Jesus says that even unworthy friends will meet the needs of their neighbor if the neighbor is persistent.

In Jesus' story, you are the neighbor with a need, and God is the friend. But God is not like the friend in the story, because God never says "Don't bother me." God is anxious to answer our prayers.

There are times, however, when it feels as if God is behaving much as the friend in Jesus' story. Remember, this is a feeling and not reality. Our feelings are not always accurate indicators of reality.

God is always anxious to meet your needs as expressed in prayer, whether or not you feel it, but it is also true that God sometimes delays His answers. It is important that we persist in prayer when God delays His answer. I prayed one prayer for twenty years before that prayer was answered.

Years ago I taught high school Bible classes at a Christian boarding school in south Texas. There was a young man at that school whom everyone loved. We'll call him Ted. Ted had unmanageable red hair, freckles, and an infectious smile. His pleasant disposition made him a favorite of faculty and students alike.

As graduation approached during his senior year, the excitement of Ted's impending reception of a high school diploma was magnified by the fact that he would be the very first person in his family ever to accomplish this milestone. He longed to share his joy with his family.

Ted purchased and mailed invitations to his friends and extended family. He bought an oversized invitation for his parents and sent it with a hand-written note of his love for them. He encouraged them to attend and share in his achievement.

Graduation at this school was no small affair. The celebration began on Friday evening, continued with meetings Saturday morning and afternoon, and culminated in commencement exercises on Saturday night. Ted expected his parents to attend all the meetings.

Friday night came and went, but no parents. I saw Ted's disappointment and attempted to comfort him. "They live 250 miles away. Perhaps they got a late start. They'll be here tomorrow."

Saturday morning came, but Ted's parents were still no-shows. As the events of the day came and passed, it was apparent that they simply weren't coming.

After one meeting, Ted's disappointment became more than he could handle. I saw him run across campus to his dormitory. As soon as I was able, I followed.

I went to Ted's room and knocked. It was locked, but I was convinced he was in there, so I knocked again. Finally, I went to the dean and got the passkey to let myself in.

I found Ted sitting in the middle of the floor in his dormitory room, sobbing. His entire body convulsed as he wept.

I am a minister of the gospel, and I hold a graduate degree in counseling, but none of that prepared me for this moment. No one told me what to say to an eighteen-year-old boy whose parents had just refused to attend the most important day of his young life. So I sat down on the floor next to Ted, put my arm around him, and cried with him.

There were no words to say. Nothing could take away the pain.

Then Ted got up, walked over to his desk, and picked up two small Bibles. His parents had given the Bibles to him. He handed the Bibles to me and said, "Here, you take these. They haven't done me much good. Take them and give them to someone else."

I said, "I don't want your Bibles. You need them."

"Take them or I'll burn them. Take them and give them away," Ted screamed.

I said, "I'll take them, but I'm not giving them to anyone. The day will come when you will want them back. I'll keep them for you until you want them again."

"Then you'll keep them forever! I don't want them," he sobbed.

Ted graduated and left the school. I learned later that his parents had just decided not to attend his graduation. They didn't have an excuse.

Perhaps they were embarrassed about never having graduated themselves, or worse yet, maybe they just didn't care.

Ted didn't speak to his parents again. His friends lost track of him, and I had no clue as to where he was or what he was doing, but I kept his Bibles and prayed that God would reach this angry young man. I prayed this prayer for twenty years.

The years passed with no word from Ted. None of us knew that he spent time in the military and that he served at the United States Embassy in Moscow. Upon returning to civilian life, his work included everything from law enforcement to working at a United States mint, but none of us knew any of this.

Twenty years passed. In fact, it was almost twenty years to the day when I was at home writing a sermon in my office, and my phone rang. The voice on the other end of the phone said, "Pastor Tucker, do you remember me? I'm Ted."

"Of course I remember you! How are you?"

Small talk filled the next five or ten minutes. Then Ted asked, "Do you still have my Bibles?"

I turned in my office chair and looked at the bookshelves behind me. "I'm looking at them right now."

"You said I could have them back when I wanted them. Could I come to your church and pick them up?"

"Could you come to my church? Of course you can! I'll have them with me. I'd love to see you again!"

We agreed that he would attend our last service and see me after the sermon. I could hardly wait!

That week, I finished my sermon a little early during the first service, so I shared Ted's story with the congregation and asked them to pray for Ted. I asked them to pray that God would heal his pain and welcome him back home.

As the service ended and the congregation was leaving, I saw a familiar figure in the rear of the church. It was Ted. He had changed plans and attended the first service and had heard me tell his story.

We embraced at the front of the church, spent a few minutes talking, and then went to my office to retrieve his Bibles. Ted thanked me and said, "I'm not sure where all this is taking me, but at least now I'm willing to take the trip. I'm going to read these and see if I can find some answers."

The journey is still not over for Ted. I'm not sure where God will lead, but I am sure that if Ted will be open to His leading, the journey will end with Ted coming home.

I prayed for twenty years with no apparent answer. For twenty years, God was silent while I labored in prayer.

I've wondered why God took twenty years to begin to answer my prayer. Why does God delay? Does the delay suggest that God loves us less than we had hoped? Is He just too busy to worry with our needs?

Lloyd John Ogilvie retired not too long ago as the chaplain of the United States Senate, a position currently held by Barry Black. Ogilvie, in his book *Praying with Power,* writes, "When prayers seem unanswered, take it as a signal that the Lord wants to help us discover our sufficiency in Him and not what He can give us in tangible blessings."

We tend to focus on our immediate needs. The more focused we become on those needs, the less likely we are to see a larger picture.

Usually, our pain is so intense it causes us to become myopic and see only the immediate source of our pain. However, sometimes the thing upon which we are so desperately focused is not our greatest need.

God alone knows what that need really is, and God alone can meet that need. It may be God's plan to give us something far better than the thing we are currently pleading for.

Jesus appears to deal with this as He continues His discussion on persistence in prayer: " 'Which of you fathers, if your son asks for a fish, will give him a snake instead? Or if he asks for an egg, will give him a scorpion? If you then, though you are evil, know how to give good gifts to your children, how much more will your Father in heaven give the Holy Spirit to those who ask him!' " (verses 11–13).

When we ask for a fish, and God delays, it seems as though He has given us a snake instead of the fish. When we ask for an egg, and God delays, it feels as if He has given us a scorpion instead of the egg.

Perhaps you have experienced God's delay, and you may feel that God doesn't care about your pain or that God is somehow sadistic and enjoys seeing you squirm. But God never gives us bad gifts, and He never gives us anything that might harm us. He may, however, delay giving a gift we so earnestly desire so that He might give us something far better—something we need much more desperately but are completely unaware of.

The issue is whether or not we are willing to trust God. Are we willing to allow God to be God?

I like the story of the evangelist who was absent from home and his two young sons for some time. He was busy doing God's work, but he realized that his boys were in desperate need of time with him. So he called home and talked with the boys and assured them that he was going to be home very soon and that when he got home they would spend a lot of time together. What was more, he promised to take the boys to Sears and buy them a gift—anything they wanted.

Now Dad had something special in mind that he wanted his boys to have, but he wanted to increase their anticipation and involve them in the process.

Soon Dad did return home, and when he drove up into the driveway, he found his sons standing there waiting for their father. He had scarcely gotten out of the car and hugged the boys before they clamored to take the promised trip to Sears.

Dad said, "Help me get my bags inside and let me say hello to your mother, and I promise you that then we will take our trip to Sears."

The boys reluctantly relented and helped their father with his bags. They watched impatiently as Mom and Dad kissed, and then they said, "All right, now it's time to go to Sears! You promised, Dad!" So Dad loaded the boys up in the car, and off they went.

When they got to Sears, the very first thing they saw was a wooden paddle with a rubber band and a little red ball attached to the end of the rubber band. The boys got all excited and said, "This is it, Dad! This is what we want! Let's look no further, since this is the gift we want!"

Well, Dad knew that he wanted to give them something better, so he said, "I'll buy this if it is what you really want, but why don't we look around a little bit first in order to know if this is the best gift?"

The boys were dubious and said, "OK, but we know this is what we want. We're just going to waste a lot of time, but we'll look some more if you want us to."

The three of them turned a corner, and the boys saw the baseball gloves. They ran to them and said, "Dad! This is what we want! We're through looking."

Again, Dad smiled and said, "I'll buy this if it is what you really want, but why don't we look around a little bit more in order to know if this is the best gift!"

The boys said, "Dad, are you really going to buy us something, or are we just wasting time here?"

Dad assured them that they would buy something soon, and so they turned another corner.

Now the boys saw basketballs. Again they squealed, "Dad! This is what we want! Let's look no further since this is the gift we want!"

Again Dad repeated, "I'll buy this if it is what you really want, but why don't we look around a little bit first in order to know if this is the best gift!"

The boys said, "Dad, you're just going to run us around in circles all day and eventually get us out to the car without anything, aren't you!"

Dad assured the boys that they would not leave empty-handed, but the boys were growing impatient and began to doubt their father's heart.

Just then, the three of them turned one last corner, and the boys stood in slack-jawed silence as they gazed on the most beautiful sight they had ever seen. They were looking at wall-to-wall bicycles.

They were almost afraid to ask the question, but finally got out a simple, "Dad, do you think we might actually get a bicycle?"

This was what Dad had wanted to buy his boys all along, so he said, "Not just one bicycle, but two—one for each of you. Let's go pick out the two best bikes in the store!"

Later that day, after having ridden their bicycles up and down the street for hours, the oldest of the two boys stopped and called his brother over and said, "Do you realize that if we hadn't trusted Dad, right now we would be playing with two stupid wooden paddles with rubber bands?"

The boys had learned a lesson about their father's heart. They learned they could trust him to give them the very best gifts possible.

Perhaps this is what God is doing when He delays the answer to our requests. Perhaps He is waiting for us to understand that there is a better gift that we really need—a gift our Father is anxious to give. But we must first trust His heart.

God longs to give us what we truly need—not what we think we need. And what we need is the gift of Himself!

Look at what Oswald Chambers has written regarding prayer: "Our understanding of God is the answer to prayer. Getting things from God is His indulgence of us. When He stops giving us things, He brings us into the place where we can begin to understand Him. As long as we get from God everything we ask for, we never get to know Him; we look at Him as a blessing machine. Your Father knows what you have need of before you ask Him. Then why pray? To get to know your Father. It is not enough to be able to say, 'God is love.' We have to know that He is love. We have to struggle through until we do see His love and justice. Then our prayer is answered."

We pray, not just for what we might get from God, but so that we might know our Father and understand His loving heart. His great heart longs to give us so much more than the paltry things we ask of Him. He longs to give us our heart's desire; He longs to give us Himself.

New Testament scholar William Barclay wrote, "Real prayer is simply being in the presence of God. When I am in trouble, and when I go to my friend, I don't want anything from him except himself. I just want to be with him for a time, to feel his comradeship, his concern, his caring round me and about me, and then to go out to a world warmer because I spent an hour with him. It must be that way with me and God. I must go to him simply for himself."

When our children were small, we played a game that most fathers have played with their children. I'd hold some coins in my fist, and they'd sit on my lap and work to get my fingers open.

The unwritten rules of finger opening are that once a finger is open, it cannot be closed again. My daughters would work at opening my fingers until they got the coins in my hand, and then they were happy and ran away with the coins.

You've played that game with your children, haven't you? We've all played that game with God, too. We pry at His fingers to get at the coins in His hand.

We say, "Lord, my rent is due, and I don't have the money." Or, "Lord, I really need to pass this class." Or "Lord, I can't afford to lose this job." Or, "Dear God, my wife has cancer."

We tug at God's fingers so that we might get at the pennies in His hand. When God answers our prayer, we run away excited about the coins we hold.

But when we do that, we miss the most important thing. We miss the hand of God Himself. That's what prayer is about. It is about seeking and knowing the Giver of the gifts. Prayer is about knowing our Father.

Our Father—our heavenly Daddy—longs to give us so much more than we could ever ask! He longs to give us our heart's great desire. He longs to give us Himself. Pray so that you might know the Father. Pray that He might give you the gift of Himself!

Chapter Eight

What Is the Most Valuable Thing You've Ever Lost?

Based on Luke 15

What is the most valuable thing you've ever lost?

A number of pretty amazing things have been lost throughout history. For example, when Napoleon invaded Spain, it was feared that the French would rob Spain of its national treasures. So the crown jewels were hidden inside one of the walls in the royal palace.

While the French were there, they remodeled much of the palace, but the jewels were not found. When the French left, the jewels still could not be found.

Today, the crown jewels of Spain are lost, believed to be hidden somewhere inside the walls of the royal palace.

But sometimes things that are lost are found. George Sims was believed to be missing in the collapse of the World Trade Center on September 11, 2001. However, Sims turned up alive in a New York hospital in August 2002, nearly a year after the twin towers fell!

The hospital called the George Sims family and said they believed Sims was a patient there, suffering with amnesia and schizophrenia.

Family members said they believed Sims was "selling things" near the twin towers when the attacks occurred. When they did not hear from him for a few weeks, they reported him missing on October 7.

His mother says he did not remember any of his family members. Though his health is not good, Sims's mother is hopeful he will recover and tell the family about what happened to him.

Anna Sims says, "If God brought him this far back to me, he will come back the rest of the way. It will take time. I am just grateful he is alive. God worked a miracle" (Associated Press, August 27, 2002).

That which was lost has now been found!

Jesus was especially interested in finding that which was lost. That is why He spent so much time with those whom society labeled as undesirables. The proper people of the day looked down on Jesus for this and questioned His integrity for spending so much time with such a bad element.

We read of one such occasion in Luke chapter 15: "Now the tax collectors and 'sinners' were all gathering around to hear him. But the Pharisees and the teachers of the law muttered, 'This man welcomes sinners and eats with them' " (Luke 15:1, 2).

If you feel like you are a sinner, I have good news for you. Jesus still welcomes sinners! In Bible times, for a man to eat a meal with you was a great honor. Therefore, people were very picky when it came to dinner guests. They were very particular because taking a meal with someone intimated a greater acceptance and intimacy than it does today. So the fact that Jesus not only welcomed sinners but also ate with them was an alarming thing to the religious elite of the day.

Jesus, as was His custom, answered their charges by telling stories. He told three stories about lost things: "Then Jesus told them this parable: 'Suppose one of you has a hundred sheep and loses one of them. Does he not leave the ninety-nine in the open country and go after the lost sheep until he finds it? And when he finds it, he joyfully puts it on his shoulders and goes home. Then he calls his friends and neighbors together and says, "Rejoice with me; I have found my lost sheep." I tell you that in the same way there will be more rejoicing in heaven over one sinner who repents than over ninety-nine righteous persons who do not need to repent' " (verses 3–7).

While you may not personally know any shepherds, there were a lot of shepherds in Jesus' day. Shepherds depended upon their sheep, and the sheep depended upon the shepherd. To the shepherd, his sheep represented his entire livelihood. If they died, the shepherd and his family would starve. So the sheep were very important to the shepherd.

Sheep are not very smart animals. They have no way of protecting themselves because they don't have sharp claws or teeth. They aren't fast enough to run away from their enemies, and their eyesight isn't good enough to see enemies at a distance. Even if they could see their enemies, sheep really aren't smart enough to know how to get away from them.

That means that sheep are totally dependent upon a shepherd for their survival. A shepherd watches over his sheep twenty-four hours a day. He protects them from wild animals. A shepherd makes certain that sheep graze in safe pastures and drink from still waters. When sheep are injured, the shepherd cleans and treats the wounds. He knows his sheep so well that he calls each of them by name. A shepherd exercises tender care for his sheep. Contemporaries of Jesus were very familiar with this picture of a shepherd.

Jesus' story tells us that just one sheep was lost. But the shepherd left the ninety-nine and went to find his lost lamb.

Now sheep don't usually get lost on purpose. They tend to nibble their way lost. A lamb eats a clump of grass here, and then he nibbles another clump just beyond the clump he just ate, and then another and another until he finds himself away from the flock. When that happens, sheep have no idea of how to find the flock because they have no sense of direction.

Notice, however, that in the story, the sheep knows it is lost but doesn't know the way home. He didn't really intend to be lost—it just happened as he thought he was going about his business as usual.

This lost sheep represents people who are lost, know they are lost, aren't sure how they got that way, and don't know the way home. God is the shepherd. He loves that which is lost so much that He leaves the ninety-nine sheep that are safe in the fold and searches for that one lost lamb. He will not rest until He finds it, and when He does, He rejoices more over the lamb He finds than He does over the ninety-nine who were never lost!

The key here is the joy of the Father over finding a single, lost lamb. That is what He feels for you today.

You may be lost and know it, but you don't really know how to come home. The Father is searching for you, and when He finds you and brings you home, He will not reprimand you for getting lost. Instead, He will throw a party and celebrate the fact that you are safe and sound inside the fold!

The second story takes a little different twist, as we shall see: " 'Or suppose a woman has ten silver coins and loses one. Does she not light a lamp, sweep the house and search carefully until she finds it? And when she finds it, she calls her friends and neighbors together and says, "Rejoice with me; I have found my lost coin." In the same way, I tell you, there is rejoicing in the presence of the angels of God over one sinner who repents' " (verses 8–10).

Most commentators agree that it was more than just money that this woman lost. When most people get married today they wear a wedding ring. A ring not only tells others that this person is married, the ring has become a symbol of the love and commitment that exists between two people. The ring's value is often more sentimental than monetary because it symbolizes the sacred union of two lives.

In Jesus' day, when a woman married, she wore a headband. This headband was a frontlet that had ten silver coins attached to it. The coins usually hung down from the headband and rested on the woman's forehead just above her eyebrows. This frontlet was her wedding ring. It told everyone that she was married and was committed to that relationship.

Since the frontlet symbolized the completeness of that union, to lose one of the ten coins seemed to suggest that her marriage was less than whole. She was desperate to find the coin and restore the frontlet—just as desperate as someone today might be to find a lost wedding ring.

In 1965, just before his first wedding anniversary, Jack Case lost his wedding ring while water skiing at Prospect Lake in Colorado. The ring became even more precious to his wife after Case died in a plane crash in 1989.

Not too long ago the city of Colorado Springs drained the lake to reline it and later refill it again. The local news featured a story about treasure seekers with metal detectors including retired electrician Orlin Knutson, who found a 1973 Volkswagen Beetle with the keys still in the ignition in the empty lake bed.

When Case's wife, Carolyn, saw the story, she asked Knutson to look for the ring lost in 1965. A couple of days later, Knutson remarkably located the missing ring and returned it to Carolyn.

"It's a total miracle," Carolyn said.

When I read this account on the Internet, I was moved by just how important this ring had become to this woman. As a band of gold, the ring wasn't worth that much really, but what it represented was of inestimable value.

Likewise, the silver coin the woman lost was not worth that much, but what it represented was of great value. To have nine coins on the frontlet was to suggest that her marriage was not whole. So the woman swept the house clean to find it.

Notice, the coin was lost in the house, but it didn't know it was lost.

I believe there are a number of people today who are lost in the church and don't know it. The coin represents the person who is lost, and the woman represents God. The story tells us that God will not rest until He sweeps the house and finds that which is lost.

If you are in the house today—in the church—and are lost and don't even know it, rest assured that God is searching for you. He will not rest until you are found. And when He finds you, He will throw a party and rejoice that what was lost is now found.

Through these first two stories, Jesus is telling us how God relates to lost people. He does not condemn them; He does not hate them. He loves them and desperately wants them back. This is why Jesus spent so much time with people that the religious leaders of the day saw as being lost.

Jesus is still preoccupied with people who are separated from Him. He is desperate to bring them home, and when He does, He throws a party to celebrate!

The Pharisees muttered about how Jesus spent so much time with people of questionable character. And He answered them by telling stories about lost things. He did this to teach them how God relates to lost people. As the shepherd earnestly searched for the lost sheep and the woman desperately searched for the lost coin, so God anxiously searches for lost people.

So far in Luke 15, Jesus has spoken of two categories of lost people— those who are lost and know they are lost, but who don't know the way home, and those who are lost in the house and don't even know it. Neither of these two groups planned to be lost, and neither may be certain how they got that way.

But now Jesus introduces us to a third category of people who are lost from God's presence:

> Jesus continued: "There was a man who had two sons. The younger one said to his father, 'Father, give me my share of the estate.' So he divided his property between them. Not long after that, the younger son got together all he had, set off for a distant country and there squandered his wealth in wild living. After he had spent everything, there was a severe famine in that whole country, and he began to be in need. So he went and hired himself out to a citizen of that country, who sent him to his fields to feed pigs. He longed to fill his stomach with the pods that the pigs were eating, but no one gave him anything.
>
> "When he came to his senses, he said, 'How many of my father's hired men have food to spare, and here I am starving to death! I will set out and go back to my father and say to him: Father, I have sinned against heaven and against you. I am no longer worthy to be called your son; make me like one of your hired men.' So he got up and went to his father.
>
> "But while he was still a long way off, his father saw him and was filled with compassion for him; he ran to his son, threw his arms around him and kissed him.
>
> "The son said to him, 'Father, I have sinned against heaven and against you. I am no longer worthy to be called your son.'
>
> "But the father said to his servants, 'Quick! Bring the best robe and put it on him. Put a ring on his finger and sandals on his feet. Bring the fattened calf and kill it. Let's have a feast and celebrate. For this son of mine was dead and is alive again; he was lost and is found.' So they began to celebrate" (verses 11–24).

When a man died, his estate was divided among his sons. If there were two sons, as in this story, the estate would be divided into three parts, with the oldest son receiving two parts, and the youngest son receiving the third part. However, this was not done until the father was dead. For the younger son to come to the father and tell him that he wanted his portion of the inheritance before his father's death was a terrible thing. It was as though he said to his father, "I want you to die. I can't wait until you are dead! So give me my inheritance now because to me you are dead."

The father was under no obligation to do this. In fact, because this was such a great insult, the father quite possibly could have disinherited the boy. But the father loved his son so much that he did the unthinkable. He gave his son a third of his fortune and wished him well.

Having done this, no one would have blamed the father if he had considered the boy to no longer exist! But instead, he longed for the boy to return. In fact, he searched the horizon every day in hope that his son would return soon!

This story was unbelievable to the listeners of that day, but Jesus was making a point. Even those who have told God, "I hate You! I wish You were dead! I want nothing to do with You forever!" are still loved by God!

Some are bothered by the fact that the father in this story did not leave home to search for the lost boy. Why did the father just wait for the boy to come home?

Let's imagine, for a moment, that you are the father of a nineteen-year-old son who comes to you and says, "Dad, I hate you! I wish you were dead! I want nothing to do with you forever! I don't want your values, and I don't want your lifestyle, so I'm leaving home now, never to return!" And then that boy left town and went to live in Las Vegas and began living a life that was the exact opposite of the values you had taught him. What would you do?

If you were a man of wealth you could hire a couple of large men with bulging muscles and no neck to go to Las Vegas and force your son to come home. When they drag the screaming boy into the living room, you could say to him, "Now go to your room and think about what you've done and don't come downstairs until you're ready to say you're sorry!"

What would happen? Would the boy go to his room and sit and think for a few hours, and then come back down and say, "Dad, I've thought it over and I've come to realize that you were right. I was wrong to say the things I said and to do the things I did. I just hope you'll forgive me"?

Absolutely not! If you try to force a nineteen-year-old young man to forsake the lifestyle he has chosen and force him to return to your home and values, you are an absolute fool! This is not going to work! The only people who think such a plan would work have either never raised children or are in denial.

The father in Jesus' story understood this. His only hope was to wait and pray for his son to return of his own accord. You cannot force someone of that age to do much, and if you do, they will resent you.

This was not what the father wanted. He didn't just want his son to come home; he wanted the son to love him and to have a genuine relationship of father-son intimacy. This could never be accomplished by force. So the father did the right thing. He trusted all the training he had given to the boy during his formative years. He knew that if and when a crisis occurred, his son would naturally return to those childhood lessons and that they would eventually lead him home.

You see, God actively searches for those who are receptive to active searching, and He patiently waits for those for whom waiting is the best method. He will do whatever is necessary to bring the lost back home.

This father waited. It seemed like an eternity, but he waited.

The boy soon found out that party-time friends are not real friends after all! They were with him when he had money, and they left him as soon as the money was gone. When the boy reached absolute bottom, he returned to the lessons of childhood, just as the father had hoped he would.

Feeding pigs was the very worst thing a Jew could think of. Pigs are declared by Deuteronomy as being unfit for human consumption. Not only were Jews not to eat pigs, they could not even touch a pig. If they did they were excluded from entering the temple until a time of purification had been completed.

This boy had to feed pigs and touch pigs, and the pay was so bad that he had to share in the slop the pigs were fed. It was then that he realized that his father's servants had a much better life than this. He decided to go home.

He knew the way home, but he wasn't sure his father would accept him back. So he came up with this really great speech that he thought might soften his father's heart.

When the father saw his son in the distance, he did something very uncharacteristic for a man of means. Rich men did not run. They never appeared to be in a hurry because people would wait for a man of wealth. It was thought to be undignified for a man of means to run. But when the father saw his son on the horizon, he threw dignity away and ran to greet his son.

It was, no doubt, the first time the son had ever seen his father run. The first time the son saw his father run, his father was running toward him.

The son started his speech, "Father, I have sinned against heaven and you . . . " The father didn't pay attention, but gave his son a big bear hug and kissed him repeatedly.

"I really don't deserve to be called your son . . . " The father ignored him and called to the servants, "Bring the best robe in the house for my son, and sandals for his feet, and, bless his heart, he had to hock the family signet. Put a ring on my son's finger."

"Father, just make me one of your hired hands . . . " The father called to another servant, "Go kill the calf we've been fattening. We are going to throw the best party you've ever seen! This son of mine was dead and is alive again; he was lost and is found!"

Words cannot describe the father's joy! The son was overwhelmed by the reception he received from the father.

The father doesn't care about the money the boy wasted, and he doesn't even care about the terrible things the boy has done. He is consumed by overwhelming joy because his son has come home!

This is how the heavenly Father relates to those who are lost because they have chosen to be lost as an act of overt rebellion. The Father receives such a person with open arms and rejoices at his return!

It does not matter how long you've been away from the Father. It does not matter how you left—whether it was unintentional or whether it was an act of open rebellion. And it does not matter what you've done while away from the Father.

The Father wants you back! He will stop at nothing to get you back! And when you come home to Him, He is going to throw a party to beat all parties. This is because the Father longs for you with all His heart!

Max Lucado writes the story of a woman named Maria whose husband died, leaving her and her daughter, Christina, to fend for themselves in a poor neighborhood on the outskirts of a Brazilian village. Christina often spoke of going to the city to seek her fame and fortune.

Christina's dreams of an exciting life horrified Maria because she knew exactly what her daughter would have to do for a living. That's why Maria's heart broke the day she awoke to find her daughter's bed empty.

Maria quickly threw some clothes in a bag, gathered up all of her money, and bought a bus ticket to Rio de Janeiro. While waiting for the bus, Maria sat in a photograph booth and spent all the time she could making photos of herself.

Maria prayed all the way to Rio that she would be able to find her daughter. Maria knew her daughter had no way of making money, and she knew Christina was too stubborn to give up. When pride meets hunger, a person will do things that were before unthinkable.

Maria began her search. She went to bars, hotels, and nightclubs— anywhere with a reputation for streetwalkers or prostitutes. Every place she went she left her photo. Sometimes she left it taped to a bathroom mirror, or tacked to a hotel bulletin board, slipped under the edge of a glass tabletop, or taped to a wall in a telephone booth. When her money and the pictures ran out, Maria went home.

A few weeks later Christina found herself in a hotel. Her beautiful face looked tired and sad. Her dreams were now a nightmare.

Before she headed up the stairs she saw a familiar face staring at her. She blinked and realized that she was indeed looking at her mother's photograph. What was her mother's photograph doing here?

She turned it over and read the inscription, "Whatever you've done, whatever you have become, it doesn't matter. Please come home."

And she did.

And that is God's message to every prodigal today. "Whatever you've done, whatever you have become, it doesn't matter. Please come home."

Every prodigal who returns to the Father is invited into the most intimate of relationships with Him. The desires of the prodigal's heart are fulfilled.

Chapter Nine

What Is the Most Beautiful Sight You've Ever Seen?

Based on Luke 18:35–43

What is the most beautiful sight you've ever seen? For many in Cambridge, England, during World War II, the most beautiful sight had to be the stained glass windows of King's College Chapel.

The residents of Cambridge were concerned that Nazi bombs might destroy this work of art, so they broke out each little section of glass and safely stored them. Once the war was over, the windows were reassembled. Each little piece was brought back to its original beauty and secured in its proper place.

After they were reassembled, the windows once again gave the residents of Cambridge great joy. Visitors come from the world over to enjoy the beauty of the sight.

What beautiful sights do you enjoy? What is the most beautiful sight you've ever seen?

Max Lucado writes about Bob Edens, a man who had been completely blind for fifty-one years. Bob's world was one of sounds and smells, but no pictures. For five decades, this man saw only blackness.

Then doctors performed a complicated operation that changed everything for Bob. For the first time in his life, Bob Edens could see!

Bob was overwhelmed by the experience. Seeing the world for the first time left him excited, like a kid with a new toy.

Bob gushed: "I never would have dreamed that yellow is so . . . yellow. I don't have the words. I am amazed by yellow. But red is my favorite color. I just can't believe red. I can see the shape of the moon, and I like nothing better than seeing a jet plane flying across the sky leaving a vapor trail. And of course, sunrises and sunsets! And at night I look at the stars in the sky and the flashing light. You could never know how wonderful everything is" (Max Lucado, *God Came Near*, Multnomah Press, 1987, p. 13).

If you were Bob Edens, what would be the first thing you would want to see? What would you long to see? What beauty would you long to behold?

Bob's enthusiasm over the things he saw with his new eyes reminds us of a story we find in chapter 18 of Luke's Gospel. Jesus was on His way to Jerusalem. Although Passover was approaching, this journey was not just for the purpose of attending the feast. Jesus was going to Jerusalem to die. He was well aware of the purpose of this last journey, but He made the trip in spite of what awaited Him.

His impending death had to weigh heavily on His mind, but in spite of that, Jesus was able to focus on teaching and ministering to those in need.

> As Jesus approached Jericho, a blind man was sitting by the roadside begging. When he heard the crowd going by, he asked what was happening. They told him, "Jesus of Nazareth is passing by."
>
> He called out, "Jesus, Son of David, have mercy on me!"
>
> Those who led the way rebuked him and told him to be quiet, but he shouted all the more, "Son of David, have mercy on me!"
>
> Jesus stopped and ordered the man to be brought to him. When he came near, Jesus asked him, "What do you want me to do for you?"
>
> "Lord, I want to see," he replied.
>
> Jesus said to him, "Receive your sight; your faith has healed

you." Immediately he received his sight and followed Jesus, praising God. When all the people saw it, they also praised God (Luke 18:35–43).

Those who attended the feasts in Jerusalem traveled in groups for protection against thieves and other dangers they might encounter along the way. Jesus was traveling with the disciples, but others accompanied them as well. As they walked, Jesus taught.

This was one of the most common ways that teachers gave instruction in those days. They taught as they walked. Those who traveled with Jesus were pressing in—getting as close to Jesus as they could so they wouldn't miss what He was saying.

Others who could not attend the feast were lining the road to see who had decided to make the journey to Jerusalem. When the crowd recognized Jesus, they pressed closer to hear what He was saying.

A blind man who sat by the side of the road became aware of the commotion and asked someone what was happening. He was told that Jesus was passing by on His way to the Passover. Mark tells this same story in his Gospel and gives us the blind man's name—Bartimaeus. Bartimaeus means "Son of Timaeus," and Timaeus means "cherished" or "blessed."

However, Bartimaeus did not feel cherished or blessed. His father may have been blessed, but not he. He was blind. The religious leaders taught that blindness was a curse from God. Bartimaeus felt cursed, not cherished or blessed.

What must it be like to be blind? When I was a boy growing up in Forth Worth, Texas, from time to time I would ride to church with my grandparents. Often they would take a short detour to pick up a man who was blind.

His eyes appeared to be fogged over. The man couldn't even detect light. He walked with a white cane and was actually able to get around town quite well. In fact, my grandparents didn't pick him up at his house because that would have been too far out of their way. Instead, he caught a city bus to a place that was on their way to church, and then he would wait for them to come by. When we pulled up in front of him as he stood at the curb, my grandfather would call him by name and assist him into the car.

The man fascinated me! I studied his eyes and wondered what it must be like to be unable to see anything.

When I got home from church I would tie a handkerchief around my eyes and take a stick in my hand and try to walk through the house without running into anything. I discovered that I was not too good at being blind. I ran into walls, chairs, and doors. It wasn't long before I would remove the blindfold and rejoice in the ability to see.

Bartimaeus had a longing in his heart. He longed for something better—something more. He longed to be able to see. So he called out, "Jesus, Son of David, have mercy on me!"

Obviously, Bartimaeus had heard of Jesus. He knew that Jesus could do something for him. But he knew more than that. Bartimaeus knew enough to call Jesus "Son of David."

That title may not mean much to you, but it meant plenty to the people of that day. "Son of David" was one of several Messianic titles. Bartimaeus referred to Jesus by a Messianic title, thus acknowledging that Jesus was the promised Messiah. In this way, Bartimaeus made a confession of his faith in Jesus. Bartimaeus proclaimed his belief that Jesus was the Messiah, the One God had promised for the deliverance of His people.

Perhaps Bartimaeus had heard Jesus preach, or perhaps he had just heard people speak of Him. We don't know what his experience with Jesus might have been, but we do know that when he called out to Jesus for help, he addressed Him by a Messianic title.

Those around Bartimaeus tried to silence him. They were trying to hear what Jesus was saying, but this blind man was making too much noise!

Bartimaeus knew this might be his only chance to be healed, so he called out to Jesus. Bartimaeus would not be silent. He wasn't going to miss the possibility that Jesus might heal him. Bartimaeus confessed his faith in Jesus as the Messiah and cried out to Him for mercy.

Verse 38 says that Bartimaeus shouted, "Jesus, Son of David, have mercy on me." The word used here for "shouted" implies an ordinary loud shout to attract attention. When those around him tried to quiet Bartimaeus so that they could hear Jesus, Bartimaeus panicked. He was afraid that he was going to miss his opportunity to be healed, so he cried all the louder, "Son of David, have mercy on me."

The word used in verse 39 to describe the man's shouting lets us know that the intensity had increased considerably. In fact, this word tells us that Bartimaeus's shout was an uncontrollable, emotional, animal-like scream! He was desperate to be healed. His desire was intense. It was all consuming.

Bartimaeus was frantic to receive mercy. He knew the longings of his heart. He longed for Jesus' healing touch. Bartimaeus longed to be restored to what he intuitively understood he was intended to be.

Bartimaeus sensed that he was created to be more, do more, and experience more. How could he settle for less when he was intended to do and be so much more? Bartimaeus was not satisfied with his life as it was. He wanted a life worth living.

Couldn't the same be said of all of us? Couldn't it be said that we all feel the need for something better?

Bartimaeus felt the longings so intensely that he screamed for help. He screamed a desperate, emotional, top-of-his-lungs scream for the mercy of God. Have you ever experienced that level of desperation?

In Cuba, almost one hundred teenagers are reported to have intentionally injected themselves with the AIDS virus. They know, of course, that the virus will kill them in a few years because Cuba does not have access to all the latest medications used to treat AIDS.

Their motive, however, isn't suicide; it's security. In Cuba, all AIDS victims are confined to sanitariums, where they experience a level of comfort many Cubans never see. They get three full meals a day, air conditioning, no power outages, and no police. They gave themselves AIDS, they say, to be liberated from society and obligatory work.

In the early 1990s, Castro introduced a new national slogan: "Socialism or Death." These individuals were so desperate that they chose death.

Bartimaeus was a desperate man. His desperation drove him to ignore the disdainful shush of the crowd and to scream wildly for God's grace. The really good news is this: Jesus didn't look at the man as though he had lost his mind. He stopped, listened to his plea, and then gave him sight.

Jesus will do the same for you today. Whatever your level of need, whatever your level of desperation, your situation is not hopeless! There is One who can supply your deepest longings. This One can fulfill your greatest needs. This One is Jesus.

Jesus loves you too much to ignore your plea. Cry out to Him and He will supply your heart's desire. He will provide your deepest need.

When I was a graduate student in Michigan, I had the opportunity to go swimming in Lake Michigan. I'm from Texas, and the water in Lake Michigan was much colder than I had imagined. But I braved the cold and splashed around for a bit.

As dusk approached, an evening fog rolled in across the water. I was about a hundred yards from shore but could see absolutely nothing. I could see no horizon, no landmarks, no objects, or lights on shore.

I paddled about for what seemed to be an eternity in an absolute panic. I had no clue as to which direction would lead me to the shore. I was completely lost until I heard voices calling to me from the shore. I swam toward the voices until I reached the safety of land.

When we are separated from Christ, we are as blind and directionally challenged as I was that day in Lake Michigan. There is only one way out of that kind of blindness. It is to move toward the voice of Jesus.

The fog that surrounded Bartimaeus drove him to scream wildly for Jesus. Jesus heard the cry and responded. "Jesus stopped and ordered the man to be brought to him. When he came near, Jesus asked him, 'What do you want me to do for you?' " (verses 40, 41). How would you answer Jesus' question, "What do you want Me to do for you?" What would you ask for? If Jesus promised to fulfill one wish for you, what would you want Him to do?

We can imagine a lot of things that we might ask of Jesus. Fame and fortune come to mind. Health and long life might be popular choices with some. Others may prefer true love. Childless couples may want children, while parents whose children are ill may want them to be healed.

Jesus gives only the very best gifts. What do you think Jesus would view as the very best possible gift for you?

Those traveling with Jesus and those standing at the side of the road that day heard the question He posed to Bartimaeus. They all had an opinion as to what Bartimaeus should request. Everyone who saw Bartimaeus knew that he was broken, inferior, somehow incomplete. They all assumed the problem was the man's blindness.

Truthfully, blindness may not have been this man's greatest problem. We are ignorant of the condition of his heart, but Bartimaeus's greatest problem may have been spiritual.

Physical blindness is used in Scripture as a metaphor for the more serious form of blindness—spiritual blindness. Those who are spiritually blind have eyes wide open and yet see nothing. This is worst part of spiritual blindness. The sufferers cannot see their need.

Blindness leaves you unaware that your face needs to be washed or that your hair needs combing. You live in ignorance of your need. That is the problem with spiritual blindness as well. We fail to see our need.

John the Revelator addresses spiritual blindness in the last book of the Bible. In Revelation chapter 3 we find a message to a church called Laodicea. Jesus is concerned that the members of that church are suffering from spiritual blindness: " 'You say, "I am rich; I have acquired wealth and do not need a thing." But you do not realize that you are wretched, pitiful, poor, blind and naked. I counsel you to buy from me gold refined in the fire, so you can become rich; and white clothes to wear, so you can cover your shameful nakedness; and salve to put on your eyes, so you can see' " (Revelation 3:17, 18). I believe this passage describes the vast majority of people today! We believe we are on the road to self-actualization. As a nation, we have wealth, military might, and great world influence, but Jesus says that we are blind to our need.

Without Jesus we are "wretched, pitiful, poor, blind, and naked." "Wretched" means that of ourselves, we cannot live righteously. We are sinners whose best efforts, Isaiah tells us, are as "filthy rags." In an earlier chapter, we already discussed exactly what Isaiah was talking about. And for the people of Jesus' day, these "filthy rags" carried an additional taboo because to touch them would leave a person ceremonially unclean and therefore unfit to enter the temple for worship.

"Pitiful" suggests that we are weak, unable to do anything about our condition. We cannot change our natural inclinations, and we cannot save ourselves. Without Jesus we are lost with no hope for eternity.

"Poor" suggests that the things we might expect would recommend us to God are of no value. He does not value our talents, our accomplishments, or even our supposed good works done apart from His Spirit. Everything we treasure is refuse. The apostle Paul called it "dung" in one translation.

In reality, Paul used the vernacular of his day for "dung," a word we would certainly not expect our pastor to use. He did this, I believe, for shock value so that we might see how bankrupt our good works are without the sanctifying power of Jesus. Apart from Jesus we are poverty stricken, while believing we are rich.

We are rag-tag beggars crying out, "I am the wealthiest man in the world!" What fools that makes us!

"Blind" suggests spiritual blindness. We are unable to see our true condition. We tend to fool ourselves into believing that we are better off than we really are. We may compare ourselves to others and feel pretty good as long as we're careful about who we compare ourselves to. But in reality, we are blind and cannot see the truth about ourselves.

"Naked" suggests that we stand without the clothing provided by Jesus—His robe of righteousness. Anything else that we attempt to wear is, indeed, "filthy rags." We are effectively naked. Without Jesus we are lost.

But the passage also tells us that we may buy from Jesus " 'gold refined in the fire, so you can become rich; and white clothes to wear, so you can cover your shameful nakedness; and salve to put on your eyes, so you can see' " (Revelation 3:18).

"Gold refined in the fire" is a pure faith. It is absolute trust in Christ for every aspect of life. When we have a pure faith, we are wealthy.

The "white clothes" Christ offers are His righteous merits. He covers our sin with His shed blood, and we are not only forgiven but are declared to be guiltless. That white garment also changes our behavior. It changes our lives to make them look more like the life of Jesus, our Savior.

Finally, Jesus provides " 'salve to put on your eyes, so you can see' " (verse 18). Eye salve is the Holy Spirit who comes into our lives and reveals to us our true condition. We can now see things we could never see before. We have spiritual sight.

Sight does not happen just because you have functioning eyes. In order to see we must have an additional element—the mind must actually be taught to see. This is the conclusion of quantum physicist Arthur Zajonc. In his book *Catching the Light,* Zajonc describes the "entwined history of light and mind." He cites studies of recovery from congenital blindness. Although cornea transplants can grant functional use of their eyes to people who have been blind from birth, something more than light and eyes are required for the patient to see.

A corneal transplant may give a patient the "power to see," but sight is rarely achieved by anyone who has missed the critical developmental "windows" in the first years of life. It is during this time that sensory and motor skills are formed. Few ever acquire the ability to see who miss those important developmental years.

Zajonc writes: "The sober truth remains that vision requires far more than a functioning physical organ. Without an inner light, without a formative visual imagination, we are blind. . . . That inner light must flow into and marry with the light of nature to bring forth a world."

Spiritual sight requires an "inner light" as well. The Holy Spirit, our spiritual "eye salve," must teach us to see the things to which we have been blind. He teaches us to see our sinfulness, our desperate need, and Jesus' abundant provision for our need. This is spiritual sight.

We are told that we must buy gold, white clothes, and eye salve from Jesus. What do we use to "buy" these spiritual necessities? The currency of heaven is our life. When we give our life to Jesus, He gives us these spiritual blessings in return. He gives us riches beyond our wildest imagination! He gives us a life worth living! Jesus makes us whole. He gives us eternal life and new eyes to see things too beautiful for words.

Jesus opens blind eyes. That is what He did for Bartimaeus. Return with me to Bartimaeus's story:

> "What do you want me to do for you?"
> "Lord, I want to see," he replied.
> Jesus said to him, "Receive your sight; your faith has healed you." Immediately he received his sight and followed Jesus, praising God. When all the people saw it, they also praised God (Luke 18:41–43).

Jesus made the blind man see, and He will give you new eyes as well. He will give you spiritual eyesight. It may not happen overnight, but it will happen.

Virgil was fifty when he had the surgery that enabled him to see for the first time since he was a child. But Virgil's first experiences with sight were less than satisfactory. While he could make out colors and movements, organizing them into something discernable was nearly impossible. Virgil had to learn how to see. He had to learn to make sense of colors, shapes, and movements. During the time that Virgil was learning, his behavior and habits were still those of a blind man.

Virgil's story is told by Oliver Sacks in his book *An Anthropologist on Mars*. Dr. Sacks concludes, "One must die as a blind person to be born again as a seeing person. It is the interim, the limbo . . . that is so terrible."

Jesus gives sight to the blind. For most of us sight comes slowly as the Holy Spirit teaches us to make sense of the shapes and colors around us. Day by day, we become accustomed to using our spiritual eyes. Day by day, our lives benefit from seeing things that before were invisible.

While most spiritual sight comes slowly, Jesus enables us to see one sight almost immediately. What do you think we are first able to see when the eye salve of the Holy Spirit is applied to our eyes?

When Bartimaeus received his sight, what was the first thing he saw? He saw the face of Jesus. Bartimaeus saw the face of his Redeemer, his Healer; the One who made him whole. No doubt, that was the most beautiful sight he had ever seen!

Today, when you receive spiritual eyesight, the best thing about your restored vision is that you get a view of Jesus that you never had before. You see Him as He is, in all His beauty and in all His glory. You will see the face of Jesus, and that is the most beautiful sight you will ever see!

That sight—the sight of Jesus—changes everything. When you see Jesus and His beauty, you immediately become aware of your own ugliness apart from Him. You see His righteousness and become aware of your own unrighteousness. You see His gentleness and become aware of your own brutality.

When you see Jesus, you notice the contrast with yourself, and that contrast points out your need. When you confess that need, Jesus reaches out to you and heals you. He forgives your sins, changes your life, and makes you a new person. He gives you a life worth living. From that day on, you see the world through different eyes. You see things you never saw before.

Many years ago a little girl was blinded as an infant as the result of an accident. And though she lived to be more than ninety years of age, she never saw anything. This girl grew up to become a beloved "saint" of American Christianity. Her name was Fanny Crosby, and she wrote many popular Christian songs, hymns, and choruses. When she was only eight years old, she wrote:

> Oh, what a happy child I am, although I cannot see.
> I am resolved that in this world, contented I will be.
> How many blessings I enjoy that other people don't.
> To weep and sigh because I'm blind—I cannot, and I won't.

What enabled an eight-year-old girl to develop such an attitude? Truthfully, she could see more clearly than the vast majority of people because she had spiritual eyesight. Fanny Crosby saw the world through spiritual eyes. She saw a picture of Jesus that most sighted people cannot see because they are looking through the wrong eyes.

You need spiritual eyes today. If you are living life apart from Jesus, you suffer from the worst kind of blindness. You suffer from spiritual blindness.

Physical blindness is a terrible thing. Physical blindness robs you of a view of the world and the sight of the faces of the people you love, and it means you are more apt to run into chairs, walls, and doors.

But spiritual blindness robs you of the most beautiful sight in the universe—the sight of the face of Jesus. Sufferers of spiritual blindness are at risk of losing eternity with Jesus—an eternal separation from God. It is a condition much worse than physical blindness.

Jesus offers to heal your blindness today. He promises to open your eyes to the real world—the spiritual world. When Jesus gives you spiritual sight, you will see the most beautiful sight you have ever seen. You will see the face of Jesus Himself.

Chapter Ten

How Does It Feel to Know You've Been Accepted?

Based on Luke 19

Baseball great Keith Hernandez has an unfulfilled longing. Hernandez is a lifetime .300 hitter. His skill as a fielder has won numerous Golden Glove awards. Hernandez won a batting championship for having the highest batting average, a Most Valuable Player award in his league, and even the World Series. Yet, something is missing from Keith's highlight reel.

With all his accomplishments, Hernandez has missed out on something crucially important to him—his father's acceptance and recognition that what he has accomplished is valuable. Gary Smalley and John Trent, in their book *The Gift of Honor*, share Keith's story:

> One day Keith asked his father, "Dad, I have a lifetime 300 batting average. What more do you want?"
>
> His father replied, "But someday you're going to look back and say, 'I could have done more.' "

Keith Hernandez has an empty place in his heart—a longing that is yet to be filled. Hernandez longs for acceptance from his father.

Do you long for acceptance? Do you long to know that someone special believes in you, is proud of you, or values who you are or what you've done?

I don't know of anyone who has never felt the sting of rejection, the pain that comes from knowing that someone believes you don't really measure up. We are all acquainted with those feelings, but how does it feel to be accepted? How does it feel to know that the person who means the most to you in the world accepts you as you are?

Luke tells of a man who discovered what it felt like to be accepted in this unconditional way:

> Jesus entered Jericho and was passing through. A man was there by the name of Zacchaeus; he was a chief tax collector and was wealthy. He wanted to see who Jesus was, but being a short man he could not, because of the crowd. So he ran ahead and climbed a sycamore-fig tree to see him, since Jesus was coming that way.
>
> When Jesus reached the spot, he looked up and said to him, "Zacchaeus, come down immediately. I must stay at your house today." So he came down at once and welcomed him gladly.
>
> All the people saw this and began to mutter, "He has gone to be the guest of a 'sinner.'"
>
> But Zacchaeus stood up and said to the Lord, "Look, Lord! Here and now I give half of my possessions to the poor, and if I have cheated anybody out of anything, I will pay back four times the amount."
>
> Jesus said to him, "Today salvation has come to this house, because this man, too, is a son of Abraham. For the Son of Man came to seek and to save what was lost" (Luke 19:1–10).

In the last chapter, we looked at the story of how Jesus, on His way into Jericho, healed blind Bartimaeus. Afterwards, Jesus entered Jericho. And as He was passing through the city, He met Zacchaeus.

Jericho is located in a fertile valley by the Jordan River. It had a strategic military importance because it commanded the approach to Jerusalem and the river crossings for those coming from the East. New Testament scholar William Barclay tells us that the city was like a garden; it was known for its palm trees, balsam groves, roses, and dates. Jericho contained some of the most fertile land in Palestine. That meant that Jericho was a wealthy city, and that made it a prime target for Roman taxation.

Zacchaeus was the head of the tax collectors. The Romans installed a system of taxation that did little to prevent abuse. The Romans would sell the right to collect taxes to the highest bidder. Then they set an amount of taxes that they expected from that area. Once the man who had purchased the right to collect taxes had paid Rome its quota, everything else he collected was his to keep. So, the tax collector set the tax rates.

Usually, the tax collector was a man who lived in that region and knew the people there. He would have grown up with the people, so he knew what their assets were and if they were trying to hide anything. He might say to Joshua, "I know you have a hundred sheep hidden up in the hills outside Jericho that you haven't paid taxes on. It's time to pay up!"

The people hated tax collectors, and not just because they hated to pay taxes. Tax collectors had unbridled power and were ruthless and dishonest. It was legalized robbery! But even that was not the worst part. The worst part was that the people who collected the taxes were their fellow countrymen, collecting for the hated Romans! The people felt as though tax collectors were traitors who placed a greater value on money than on their homeland and fellow citizens.

This is how people felt about Zacchaeus. In fact, Zacchaeus was probably the most hated man in town.

For Zacchaeus to go out into the streets to see Jesus was quite a risk. Because he was a diminutive man, larger men would have no trouble knocking him down. In fact, they would have taken great delight in doing so. Zacchaeus knew he would be bruised and possibly even bleeding that evening, but he risked it to see Jesus.

What made Zacchaeus take an interest in Jesus? The truth was, he was lonely. His wealth had become of little importance to him. The search for money had left him empty and perhaps feeling a bit guilty.

What Zacchaeus really wanted was to know that he mattered. He wanted to be respected, to be loved and accepted. Zacchaeus was willing to risk everything to find acceptance. He had heard that Jesus welcomed tax collectors and sinners, and he wondered if Jesus might accept him. Zacchaeus longed to feel the warmth of human kindness.

It was true that he had no one to blame but himself for his lack of popularity. He had demonstrated the ability to harden his heart against pleas for mercy from those who found it difficult if not impossible to pay their taxes. He had selfishly acted in his own self-interest while ignoring the needs of others.

The truth is, the worst person you know—the most dishonest, unlikable person you know—longs for the warmth of human kindness. Everyone longs for acceptance from someone.

Abraham Maslow tells us that there are basic human needs that each of us needs to have met. Among the most basic of those needs are physical needs such as food and shelter. Then we have needs for safety, security, consistency, and stability at home with our families, and in society in a chaotic world. Finally, we all need love and esteem.

Human beings are motivated to satisfy these cravings. If these basic needs are unmet, Maslow said, human beings cannot act unselfishly.

We all long for acceptance and love. Zacchaeus was desperate to be loved and accepted. He was willing to risk the anger and the ridicule of the crowd for the opportunity to see the Man he had heard would welcome someone like himself.

But Zacchaeus was short, and the people took great delight in not allowing him to see Jesus. In a desperate move, Zacchaeus ran ahead, perhaps by a back alley, and climbed a tree whose branches overhung the road Jesus was walking on.

The sight of what happened next must have been comical to everyone. Jesus stopped at the base of the tree and looked up. There sat Zacchaeus! The people must have laughed to see him there! They made jokes at his expense and shouted insults at him.

But Jesus treated this outcast of society with respect. He said, "Zacchaeus, come down immediately. I must stay at your house today."

Imagine the shock Zacchaeus must have experienced! Not only had Jesus stopped and noticed him, but He hadn't made fun of him for climbing the tree. Jesus treated him with respect and dignity. Jesus even knew his name!

Jesus didn't say, "Hey, little guy in the tree! Come down here. I'm staying at your place today." Jesus called him by name—Zacchaeus.

People like it when you know their name. You honor a man when you remember his name. And Zacchaeus felt honored that Jesus called his name.

But the most amazing thing to Zacchaeus was that Jesus wanted to stay at his house! No one ever wanted to stay at his house! He was an outcast. Most people would cross the road in order to avoid making eye contact with Zacchaeus. They would not address him in public. They might curse him behind his back, but they wouldn't speak directly to him unless it was absolutely necessary. But not only did Jesus address him in public and call him by name, He declared that He would stay with him in his home.

For a man longing for acceptance, this was wonderful. Jesus had far exceeded Zacchaeus's expectations. Jesus went out of His way to say, "Others may reject you, but I accept you just as you are. You are loved, forgiven, and accepted." Zacchaeus's basic human need for love and esteem had been met.

God loves those no one else loves. He loves those others reject. If He could love someone like Zacchaeus, you'd better believe He loves you!

Michael was a high school athlete who was very concerned about what others thought about him. So when Brian, a developmentally challenged student, started hanging out around Michael, it was a bit embarrassing.

Brian's dad had left him and his mom when Brian was just five years old. When his dad left, he told Brian it was because he couldn't deal with a son like him anymore. Then he walked out, and Brian never saw him again.

Brian longed for acceptance. Michael was a Christian and decided he would be nice to Brian even though everyone else teased Brian relentlessly. Brian didn't realize at times that the kids were laughing at him and not with him. Finally, Michael told his friends to "knock it off." The teasing stopped for a short time, but then picked up again. Brian was now Michael's pal. After all, no one had ever taken up for him before!

So Mike invited Brian over to play video games. While they were playing, Brian asked questions like, "Michael, where do you go to church?" And, "Michael, how come you're not like some of the other kids at school?"

Michael's girlfriend whispered to Michael, "Brian is ready to be introduced to Jesus." So Michael took Brian aside and told him about Jesus and His offer of salvation. Brian accepted Jesus as his Savior by repeating a very simple prayer as Michael led him.

After the prayer, Michael looked at Brian and asked, "Where is Jesus now?" Brian pointed to his heart and said, "Right in here." There were tears in his eyes. Brian may have been developmentally challenged, but he understood the most important theology of the Bible: "Jesus loves me, this I know. For the Bible tells me so."

Brian and Zacchaeus had been rejected by others but were accepted by God. So too, are you. God loves you and accepts you regardless of who you are or what you've done. Jesus' treatment of Zacchaeus tells you that God loves you!

Distinguished psychiatrist Viktor Frankl said that man's greatest search was a search for meaning. And he added that meaning usually was found in loving and being loved by other people. Human beings long to be loved and accepted.

However, that means that we place ourselves at risk. If we depend on other human beings to fulfill our needs for love and acceptance, we may be in trouble. It has been my experience that human acceptance is conditional and is often based on questionable criteria. Here's what I mean.

Mary was nervous about meeting her boyfriend's parents for the first time. She wanted to look her absolute best. As she glanced at herself in the mirror, she noticed her shoes looked a little dingy, so she gave them a fast swipe with the paper towel she had used to blot her breakfast bacon.

When she arrived, the parents greeted her—and so did their spoiled, cranky poodle, Cleo. The dog got a whiff of the bacon grease on Mary's shoes and followed her around all evening.

At the end of the evening, as Mary was getting ready to leave, her boyfriend's parents said, "Cleo really likes you, dear, and she is an excellent judge of character. We are delighted to welcome you into our little family."

Understand that the basis of this family's acceptance of Mary was a spoiled poodle's love for the smell of bacon on Mary's shoes! The love and acceptance we receive from others is often conditional and based on questionable criteria. In essence they say: "I'll love you if you are pretty" or "I'll love you if you are smart" or "I'll love you if you are rich and successful."

Whatever happened to "I love you no matter what"?

Dr. Joe Harding told the story of a man who had found that kind of unconditional love from his wife. This man decided to ask his boss for a raise in salary. It was Friday. He told his wife that morning what he was going to do. All day the man felt nervous and apprehensive. Late in the afternoon he summoned the courage to approach his employer. To his delight, the boss agreed to give him a raise.

The man arrived home to a beautiful table set with their best china. Candles were lighted. His wife had prepared a festive meal. He figured that someone from the office had tipped her off! Finding his wife in the kitchen, he told her the good news. They embraced and kissed, then sat down to a wonderful meal. Next to his plate the man found a beautifully lettered note. It read: "Congratulations, darling! I knew you'd get the raise! These things will tell you how much I love you."

While on his way to the kitchen to get dessert he noticed a second card on the floor where it had fallen from his wife's pocket. Picking it up, he read: "Don't worry about not getting the raise! You deserve it anyway! These things will tell you how much I love you."

Total acceptance! Total love.

Her love for him was not contingent upon his success at work. If he were to fail there—if were to be rejected by his boss—he would be all the more accepted at home.

When someone is successful, good-looking, rich, talented, or popular, everyone likes him or her. Acceptance is easy to come by for such "beautiful people." But when you are down and out or when you are not one of the "beautiful people" or when you've made a few mistakes along the way, it seems that no one loves you. Everyone finds it easy to reject you.

To be loved and accepted when you are a failure or when you do things that are wrong is a true miracle. I believe that the greatest miracle that Jesus performs today is the miracle of loving and accepting those whom everyone else rejects. This is Zacchaeus's story.

When Jesus came through town that day, Zacchaeus ran ahead of the crowd, climbed a tree, and watched for Jesus to walk by. He wondered if it was true that Jesus would accept a man like him. Soon his questions were answered. "When Jesus reached the spot, he looked up and said to him, 'Zacchaeus, come down immediately. I must stay at your house today' " (verse 5). Jesus accepted Zacchaeus. Something wonderful happens when we are loved that way. Something wonderful happens when we know we are accepted just as we are. When we are loved and accepted, there is born in our heart a desire to change.

Do you remember the movie *As Good As It Gets*? Jack Nicholson played a severely neurotic man who was extremely self-centered, selfish, and obnoxiously rude. He fell in love with a waitress played by Helen Hunt, and she loved him, too—in spite of his selfish, demanding, neurotic mannerisms.

At a very tender moment in the film, Nicholson looks into Helen Hunt's eyes and says, "You make me want to be a better man."

That's what happens when we meet Jesus. When we feel His warmth and acceptance, He makes us want to be better men and women. And that's what happened to Zacchaeus.

Jesus went home with Zacchaeus that day, and the love and acceptance demonstrated by that act changed him. Jesus' love made Zacchaeus want to be a better man.

Those who had rejected Zacchaeus doubted that any good could come from this. They complained about Jesus spending time with the trash of society.

But Zacchaeus was a changed man.

> All the people saw this and began to mutter, "He has gone to be the guest of a 'sinner.' "
> But Zacchaeus stood up and said to the Lord, "Look, Lord! Here and now I give half of my possessions to the poor, and if I have cheated anybody out of anything, I will pay back four times the amount."

Jesus said to him, "Today salvation has come to this house, because this man, too, is a son of Abraham. For the Son of Man came to seek and to save what was lost" (verses 7–9).

When Zacchaeus knew he was loved and accepted, it made him want to be a better man. Loving acceptance changed his life. He gave away half of his wealth to those he had previously terrorized—the poor.

Can you imagine the shocked looks on the faces of these people when Zacchaeus, the hated tax collector, came to their house to give them money? The other half of his possessions would be given away as well because Zacchaeus offered to pay restitution to those he had cheated.

Actually, this was far beyond what the law required. New Testament scholar William Barclay tells us that because Zacchaeus had voluntarily confessed this theft, the law required that he pay back the amount stolen plus 20 percent. A four-fold repayment was required only when there was no confession and the robbery was "a deliberate and violent act of destruction." Zacchaeus chose to go above and beyond the bare requirement of the law. All of this would certainly bankrupt Zacchaeus. But he was no longer motivated by wealth. His life had been changed by the power of love.

Love changes us. It makes us unselfish. But because human love is so fickle, we must find a more reliable source of loving acceptance. That reliable source is Jesus. If Jesus could love and accept a scoundrel like Zacchaeus, He can certainly love and accept you! And when you understand that Jesus loves you and accepts you, His love changes you. It makes you the person you were intended to be.

We love because He first loved us (see 1 John 4:19). That's how it feels to be accepted!

Maxie Dunham tells a story that illustrates the power love has to change people. It seems that the American Red Cross was gathering supplies—medicine, clothing, food, and the like—for the suffering people of a war-torn region of Africa. The volunteers found a letter inside one of the boxes that showed up at a collection center. The letter said, "We have recently been converted, and because of our conversion we want to help. We won't ever need these again. Can you use them for something?"

Inside the box were several Ku Klux Klan sheets. They cut the Klan robes up into strips and used them for bandages to be used to help heal the wounds of black people in Africa! From symbols of hatred to bandages of love! That's what happens when you know that God loves and accepts you. It changes you.

That great preacher John Wesley was stopped late one night by a bandit. The man grabbed the bridle of Wesley's horse and threatened to kill him if he didn't hand over all his money. John Wesley quickly obliged, but the thief was disappointed with how small his take was.

As the robber started to leave, Wesley cried, "Stop! I have something more to give you." The robber was startled, but turned back.

Wesley said, "My friend, you may live to regret this sort of a life in which you are engaged. If you ever do, I beseech you to remember this, 'The blood of Jesus Christ, God's Son, cleanses us from all sin.'"

The robber turned and ran away.

Years later, as an elderly John Wesley concluded an evening preaching service, a well-dressed man pressed forward to speak with him. It was the man who had robbed him years ago. He was now a well-to-do tradesman in the city. He had heeded Wesley's words and accepted the loving forgiveness of Jesus.

The former robber embraced Wesley and cried, "To you, dear sir, I owe it all." Wesley replied softly, "Not to me, but to the precious blood of Christ."

That is how it feels to be accepted—completely loved and accepted by God. It changes you into the person you were always intended to be.

Chapter Eleven

What Is the One Thing You Absolutely Must Have?

Based on Luke 22

As we have studied the Gospel of Luke, one thing is clear. Whatever your needs, whatever your sorrows, whatever your crisis, whatever your inadequacies, God has made provision for you. He has anticipated your needs and has lovingly made provision for those needs. He understands your heart's desire, and He alone can satisfy that desire.

I have a friend whose father made provision for him. While my friend was a teenager, his father was converted to Christianity. The man was a farmer, and although he was not a wealthy man, he was a landowner, so there were some assets belonging to the family. When my friend's father was converted, he felt a call to preach, so he gave everything he possessed to the church and became a pastor.

But this man's concern for his children—a son and a daughter—caused him to enter into an agreement with the church. In exchange for the man's farm, the church agreed to pay for those two teenagers to go to college at a church-owned college.

This man no longer had property or very much money, but he had made provision for the education of his two children. Their expenses at college were cared for.

What are your needs? Your heavenly Father has made provision for you.

Are you orphaned or estranged from family? God has promised to be a "father to the fatherless" (Psalm 68:5).

Have you been widowed or divorced? God has promised to be your mate. Ladies, He has promised to be your husband. Men, this means that God will be your wife. God will lovingly enter into relationship with you and provide for you an intimacy that will ensure that you will never be alone.

Are you ill? God has promised healing for your body. God may choose to heal you immediately. Or He may heal you over time with medicine, surgery, or treatments. Or He may heal you on resurrection morning. But God will heal you if you ask.

There is, however, one need we have not yet mentioned. This may be your greatest need. It could be the one thing you absolutely cannot do without. God has promised a relationship of love, forgiveness, and acceptance. You can have this relationship with God Himself. It is the greatest need in the world, and God has made provision for that need as well.

So that we might never forget the provision made by our Father, Jesus left us with some powerful symbols—reminders that God's provision is more than adequate to meet our need.

It was Passover season, and Jesus had come to Jerusalem one last time. The male inhabitants of Palestine were required to attend certain feasts in Jerusalem if at all possible. Passover was the greatest of these required feasts.

Jesus was in Jerusalem with His disciples during Passover, but He knew that He would not see the conclusion of this Passover. He knew He was going to die. Jesus longed to eat one final Passover meal with His disciples, so He sent two disciples into the city to find a room God had provided for this purpose.

As they had been instructed, the disciples found a man carrying a large jar of water. This was not an ordinary sight, because carrying water was a woman's work. Men did not do this, but the disciples found a man doing a woman's work and followed him home. They went to the master of the house and said, "The Teacher says, 'Where is the guest room where I may eat the Passover with My disciples?'" (see Luke 22:11).

The disciples were shown a large upper room. They simply mentioned "the Teacher," and the owner of the house provided a room for His use. There the disciples prepared for the Passover.

During the Passover meal, Jesus instituted a wonderful ceremony that was to be repeated by His followers throughout the centuries until His return. This ceremony celebrates the loving provision of our Lord for the forgiveness of our sins. Luke describes the events of that night:

> And he said to them, "I have eagerly desired to eat this Passover with you before I suffer. For I tell you, I will not eat it again until it finds fulfillment in the kingdom of God."
>
> After taking the cup, he gave thanks and said, "Take this and divide it among you. For I tell you I will not drink again of the fruit of the vine until the kingdom of God comes."
>
> And he took bread, gave thanks and broke it, and gave it to them, saying, "This is my body given for you; do this in remembrance of me."
>
> In the same way, after the supper he took the cup, saying, "This cup is the new covenant in my blood, which is poured out for you. But the hand of him who is going to betray me is with mine on the table. The Son of Man will go as it has been decreed, but woe to that man who betrays him" (verses 15–22).

Jesus made provision for you through His broken body and His shed blood. His loving sacrifice paid the price for your sins.

At that Last Supper with His disciples, Jesus said, "This cup is the new covenant in my blood, which is poured out for you" (verse 20). A covenant is a relationship between two parties; it is a promise or a binding contract. When a couple decides to get married they are said to enter into the covenant of marriage.

Jesus has entered into a covenant relationship with you. He has claimed His church as His chosen bride—a relationship that will be celebrated in heaven at a feast called "The Marriage Feast of the Lamb."

In the Old Testament, there was a covenant between the Israelites and God. As their end of the bargain, the Israelites chose to offer obedience to God. They promised to be obedient, and God promised to provide salvation. The problem is that no human being has ever been able to keep our end of that bargain. We are incapable of living a sin-free life. Our sin has broken the relationship with God. God could not bear the thought of that relationship being broken, so, as He had planned from the beginning, He entered into a plan of rescue.

To help those who lived during Old Testament times to understand and accept His rescue offer, God devised a system of worship that would point to the coming atonement to be made in their behalf. He instituted a system of sacrifices and festivals so that people might accept, by faith, the provision that Jesus would make for every sinner. Jesus would make atonement for our sins.

As He ate that last Passover meal with His disciples, what Jesus was saying was this: "By My life and by My death I have made possible a new relationship between you and God. You are sinners, but because I will die for you, a new, saving relationship is available for you with God."

It cost the life of Christ to restore the lost relationship between God and man. Because of that sacrifice, you can have salvation today and enter into a new, dynamic relationship with God. The deepest longings of your heart can be satisfied through the death of Jesus on Calvary.

So we would never forget, Jesus instituted a service—a memorial service, if you will—that employs symbols designed to remind us of Heaven's provision for our need. These symbols are powerful emblems of reconciliation. The emblems remind us that our salvation is never about us; it is always about Jesus. It doesn't matter how good or how bad we've been. It matters only how good Jesus is. And believe me, Jesus is plenty good enough to win our salvation.

Let's look at the emblems. First, before the meal, Jesus washed His disciples' feet. It was the custom in those days for a servant to meet guests at the door, remove their sandals, and wash their feet. But there was no servant when Jesus and the disciples entered the upper room. This duty should have fallen to one of the disciples, but their pride would not allow them to perform such menial service. Jesus served as their example and washed their feet. Thus Jesus used water as a symbol of cleansing and reconciliation.

You will remember that John the Baptist—and later, Jesus' disciples—involved new believers in the moving ceremony of baptism. This ceremony is a memorial of the death, burial, and resurrection of Jesus, representing the death of our old, sinful nature and our resurrection into newness of life in Christ.

The Bible tells us "the wages of sin is death" (Romans 6:23). Everyone who has ever sinned deserves the full penalty of the law of God, which is eternal separation from God. Because the source of life is to be found in Jesus, and Jesus is inseparable from the Father, to be separated from God is to die. But Jesus paid that penalty for us. He gave His perfect life on the cross so that we might remain connected to the source of life. Jesus paid our wage; He paid our penalty. Because Jesus died, was buried, and was then resurrected, you never need experience eternal death.

Baptism is a memorial of Jesus' death, burial, and resurrection. The washing of feet, in association with the Communion service, reminds us of our rebirth experience with Jesus. It reminds us of the day we plunged into the watery grave of baptism for the remission of sins.

The next emblem is bread. Bread was an essential element of food in the ancient world. It was the staff of life, being eaten at virtually every meal. Bread represents the body of Christ. Jesus broke the bread, or literally, tore it in pieces and gave it to the disciples. The body of Christ was broken, and a measure given to you.

The bread eaten at the Passover did not have yeast. This was to symbolize the hurried departure of Israel from Egypt. The Israelites left in such a hurry they didn't have time to let the bread rise.

In Scripture, yeast is used to symbolize sin. The bread representing the body of Jesus is without yeast just as Jesus' life was without sin. That sinless life was broken for you.

Finally, wine was used to symbolize the blood of Jesus. His blood was shed on the cross. We read in Hebrews that unless blood is shed, sins cannot be taken away. This is because blood represents life.

Jesus willingly surrendered His life in payment for our sins. This means you can be forgiven and granted unlimited access to Jesus, the source of life, if you will accept His shed blood in payment for your sins.

Every time we take a bath, eat bread, or drink the juice of the grape, we are to be reminded of what Jesus has done for us. Jesus said, "Do this in remembrance of Me," and so we are to celebrate His death, burial, and resurrection through this service.

These are the emblems Jesus gave us, and this is the ceremony He established for us, that we might never forget the provision He made for our greatest need. Jesus' sacrifice won our salvation, thus providing eternal fellowship with Him.

Your heart longs for this type of intimate relationship. Jesus created this desire in you. Since Jesus designed this desire in your heart, He has made provision to satisfy your heart's desire. And He reminds us of this gracious provision through water, bread, and wine.

As humans, we seem to have an incredible ability to forget things. We can even forget things as important as how our salvation was won. So Jesus left powerful reminders of His sacrifice. We use the emblems of water, bread, and wine in the Lord's Supper so that we might remember Jesus and His gracious provision for us.

Remembering is a sacred act. It is an act of devotion. Remembering, or meditating, on Jesus' sacrifice is an act of worship. The emblems of the Lord's Supper help us remember our salvation.

The emblems of the Lord's Supper are powerful emblems of reconciliation. First, they reconcile us to God. As, in faith, you accept these emblems and what they represent, your sins are forgiven. By grace through faith, you are the recipient of eternal life through Jesus Christ our Lord. The wall of separation between you and God has been torn down. You now have access to the God of your salvation through the body and blood of Jesus. The ruptured relationship is healed.

In addition, another form of reconciliation can take place with these emblems. I have seen water, bread, and wine serve as healing agents in the relationship between brothers and sisters in Christ, and even between husbands and wives.

Jim and Alice had done just about everything possible to destroy their marriage. Alice had been harsh, demanding, and critical of her husband. She was driven to succeed at work, so she tended to ignore her husband. Through the years, she destroyed his love for her.

Jim was very laid back. He wasn't particularly motivated to succeed, and that drove Alice crazy. But the more Alice pushed him to succeed, the more Jim resented his wife.

Jim worked for an airline, and through his work he met another woman. He began to develop an interest in her. She worked for the same airline, but in another city, so they communicated by email and by telephone. Occasionally, the two would use the free flights they acquired at work in order to meet each other.

This woman made Jim feel alive again. Alice thought he was lazy and stupid, but the other woman thought he was smart and respected him. Eventually, Jim was involved in an affair.

Alice suspected that something was up. Alice worked for the same airline as Jim, so she began to check up on him. She learned about the trips to meet his lover and found some rather incriminating email communication with the other woman. She confronted Jim, but he denied the whole thing.

The marriage was deteriorating rapidly.

Valentine's Day was approaching when Alice had the feeling that something was about to happen. Call it woman's intuition, but Alice just felt that the two lovers had planned a get-together over Valentine's Day. So she did some quick checking on the airline computer and guessed which flight the other woman might use to visit Jim. She went to the airport and inconspicuously waited and watched. Soon, she saw Jim walk up to the gate holding flowers, a box of candy, and a card.

Just before the passengers got off the plane, Jim saw Alice.

"What are you doing here?"

"I've come to meet your girlfriend. I want to meet the woman who means so much to you!"

At that moment, the first few passengers began to file out of the jetway. Alice said, "Which one is she? Let me guess."

Alice approached a woman and called her by the name she had seen on the emails, and the woman answered. Alice had guessed correctly. Jim was flabbergasted!

Alice said, "Jim, come give her your presents!" Then she turned to the woman and said, "I hope you enjoy these. They're more than I'll probably get. Come on, Jim, give her the card, too!"

Talk about an uncomfortable situation!

Believe it or not, that incident didn't end the marriage. Friends referred Jim and Alice to me for counseling. We had a number of very uncomfortable sessions together, but eventually, I saw the Holy Spirit at work. Jim and Alice both began to soften, and both asked for forgiveness.

Forgiveness is not always easy to give—especially when the wounds are as deep as they were for Jim and Alice. To help cement their expressions of forgiveness, we had Communion in my office one evening.

Following Jesus' example, they washed each other's feet. This act not only demonstrates a servant's heart, but the water is also reminiscent of the waters of baptism that wash away our sins.

Then I read Scripture as the two of them ate the bread and drank the wine—the emblems of Christ's broken body and shed blood.

> After taking the cup, he [Jesus] gave thanks and said, "Take this and divide it among you. For I tell you I will not drink again of the fruit of the vine until the kingdom of God comes."
>
> And he took bread, gave thanks and broke it, and gave it to them, saying, "This is my body given for you; do this in remembrance of me."
>
> In the same way, after the supper he took the cup, saying, "This cup is the new covenant in my blood, which is poured out for you" (verses 17–20).

Jim and Alice shared the emblems of Christ's broken body and shed blood. They experienced reconciliation with God and with each other. Then they embraced with hot tears of repentance and love.

The presence of the Holy Spirit was so strong in that room that I felt like an intruder. I excused myself, leaving the three of them—Jim, Alice, and the Holy Spirit—to experience reconciliation.

Jim and Alice are still together today, more in love than they've ever been. God reconciled them to Himself and to each other through the emblems of Christ's sacrifice.

Jesus gave us water, bread, and wine, and they are powerful symbols of reconciliation. They tell us that Jesus paid a price for us. Because of our sin, we deserve to die.

The Bible tells us that sin has a penalty, or as Paul puts it, a "wage." He says, "The wages of sin is death" (Romans 6:23). That means, if you have sinned, the death penalty has been pronounced upon your life. Everyone who has sinned has engaged in open rebellion against God, and that rebellion separates us from Him. We cannot live apart from God because He is the source of all life. So our sin separates us from God, and that results in our death.

But God's heart breaks at the thought of losing you! He cannot stand idly by and watch as our sin separates us from His presence and results in our eternal death. Yet, He can't just ignore our sin. Justice is an important part of God's character, and to deny justice would be to violate His own true self. He could not do that.

So Jesus came to pay our penalty on our behalf. Thus, the requirements of justice were met, and a way of reconciliation was provided.

The last half of Romans 6:23 continues, "But the gift of God is eternal life in Christ Jesus our Lord."

Christ's sacrifice is a gift to you. The gift is forgiveness—salvation—eternal life! The gift provides the means of reconciliation between you and God. God need not spend eternity without you since Christ has reconciled you to God.

Whenever we participate in washing the feet of fellow believers and in the Communion service, we celebrate what Christ did on the cross. We celebrate the payment that was made for our sins. We celebrate the reconciliation provided on our behalf by our Savior, Jesus Christ.

When, in faith, we receive the bread and the wine, we accept the reconciliation provided by Christ's sacrifice. We accept the gift of eternal life.

Max Lucado tells of a young man who approached his pastor at the close of a worship service and asked, "What can I do to find peace in my life?"

The pastor replied, "I'm sorry, but you're too late."

The young man was distraught. He said, "You mean I'm too late to find peace? You mean I'm too late to be saved?"

The pastor answered, "No, you're just too late to do anything about it. Jesus did everything that needed to be done two thousand years ago."

It is too late for you to do anything about your peace and your salvation. Jesus has already made provision for that. Your only duty is to accept His gracious provision. Jesus did all the work, and we get all the benefit.

Actor Kevin Bacon acted in the movie *Footloose.* The movie was very demanding physically on Bacon and required a number of stunt doubles.

When Kevin's six-year-old son saw *Footloose* for the first time he said, "Hey, Dad, you know that thing in the movie where you swing from the rafters of that building? That's really cool. How did you do that?"

Bacon said, "Well, I didn't do that part—it was a stunt man."

"What's a stunt man?" he asked.

"That's someone who dresses like me and does things I can't do."

"Oh," his son replied and walked out of the room looking a little confused.

A little later the boy said, "Hey, Dad, you know that thing in the movie where you spin around on that gym bar and land on your feet? How did you do that?"

Bacon said, "Well, I didn't do that. It was a gymnastics double."

"What's a gymnastics double?" he asked.

"That's a guy who dresses in my clothes and does things I can't do."

There was silence. Then the boy asked in a concerned voice, "Dad, what did you do?"

"I got all the glory," Bacon sheepishly replied.

That's what Jesus did for us. He did what we couldn't do so that we might stand forgiven, as clean as though we had never sinned. We know we have sinned, but that's not how God treats us when we accept the sacrifice Christ made on our behalf. Jesus did the work, and we get the benefit.

In *Leadership* magazine, Steve Winger from Lubbock, Texas, wrote about his last college test. The test was a final in a logic class known for its difficult exams.

The professor told the students they could bring as much information to the exam as they could fit on a piece of notebook paper. Of course, most students used very small writing to cram as many facts as possible on the sheet of notebook paper.

But one student found a better way. He put a piece of notebook paper on the floor next to his desk, and then had an advanced logic student stand on the paper. This student had everything he needed to be the only student in the entire class to get an A.

Someone who knew the answers did the work for him, and he got a superior grade. That we might never forget that Jesus did the work for us, He gave us the emblems of water, bread, and wine. They are to remind us that we can live forever since Jesus died in our place. That's why Jesus said, "This is my body given for you; do this in remembrance of me" (Luke 22:19).

I urge you to accept the provision Jesus made for you. Accept that He has done all the work for you. And every time you wash your feet or eat bread or drink the fruit of the vine, remember Jesus and the salvation He won for you.

Chapter Twelve

Has Anyone Ever Placed Himself at Risk for You?

Based on Luke 23

On December 26, 2004, an earthquake of 9.0 magnitude rocked the floor of the Indian Ocean, resulting in a gigantic tsunami. The waves devastated the entire region, killing over 160,000 people.

One place the tsunami hit was Phuket, Thailand. Michael Bergman of Sweden was vacationing with his family at a resort in Phuket. His wife, Cecilia, his eighteen-month-old son, Hannes, and Michael's mother were having a wonderful time until the tsunami hit.

Michael and his mother survived the ordeal and ended up in the hospital. But Hannes and Cecilia were missing. Cecilia is still missing and presumed dead.

Hannes ended up in a pile of rubble. A Thai princess, who was staying in a nearby building, spotted the boy. Like the Egyptian princess who long ago plucked Moses from the Nile, she rescued the toddler.

As the princess held the child in her arms, her heart ached for the parents. She wondered if they were still alive. She used her resources to search for the toddler's family. Once she determined that the child's father was alive and in a hospital, the princess had the boy airlifted by helicopter to be reunited with his father.

Michael Bergman was incredibly moved, saying that the princess not only saved his son but also saved his own soul. By giving him back his son, the princess saved that part of him, too.

Just as an eighteen-month-old boy was restored to his father's arms by the efforts of a princess, so you have been restored to your heavenly Father's arms by the incredible efforts of Jesus. His sacrifice has reunited you with your Father.

Luke's Gospel, chapter 22, tells us that Jesus took His disciples to a garden to pray. The garden was called Gethsemane. Most likely, it was owned by a friend who had given Jesus permission to use it whenever He needed. Jesus had taken the disciples there before. That's how Judas knew where to find them.

Jesus knew He would need this time with His Father. He came to the Garden to pray and longed to have His disciples join Him in prayer. He needed their support. But the disciples fell asleep.

No doubt, you have seen lovely paintings of Jesus as He prayed that night. Usually, they picture Him serenely kneeling with hands folded and face illumined as He looks to heaven. As lovely as this picture may be, I do not believe it is accurate. Jesus wrestled with the Father in prayer that night, sweating great drops of blood and lying face-down on the ground, digging hands full of dirt as He agonized in prayer. He cried out, " 'Father, if you are willing, take this cup from me; yet not my will, but yours be done' " (Luke 22:42).

This was no easy "now I lay me down to sleep" type of prayer. This prayer was a battleground. Jesus longed to restore you to your Father, but He understood that to do so would cause Him great anguish and pain. He knew that ultimately it would cost His life. A part of Him, the human part, cried out to be released from such a horrible price. However, Jesus resolved to remain obedient to the Father and do all that was necessary to restore us.

In the midst of all this, Judas had bargained with the priests and had arranged for Jesus to be arrested. He led the soldiers to the place he knew Jesus would be praying and betrayed the Lord with a kiss. Jesus was arrested, abused by the guards, and taken before the high priest to be tried. "Then seizing him, they led him away and took him into the house of the high priest" (verse 54).

When Jesus was taken to the home of the high priest to be tried, the Jewish leaders convened an impromptu meeting of a judicial body known as the Sanhedrin. However, in so doing, the Sanhedrin broke all its own laws.

The regulations for the procedure of the Sanhedrin are in one of the tractates of the Mishnah. The Sanhedrin was the supreme court of the Jews and was composed of seventy-one members. There were the Sadducees—a group which comprised the priestly classes. Also, the Pharisees and scribes were represented. These were the experts in the law. And then there were respected men who were elders.

The high priest presided over the court. The court sat in a semi-circle in such a way that any member could see every other member. The students of the rabbis sat at the opening of the semi-circle, facing the members of the court. These students were allowed to speak on behalf of the accused, but not against him. However, at Jesus' trial they spoke out against Jesus.

The official meeting place of the Sanhedrin was the Hall of Hewn Stone, located within the temple precincts. The decisions of the Sanhedrin were not valid unless they were reached at a meeting held in that place. Yet, for Jesus' trial, the Sanhedrin met in the residence of the high priest.

By law, the court could not meet at night nor could it meet at any of the great feasts. Yet, here the Sanhedrin was meeting at night during the Passover. The law stated that witnesses were to be examined separately when evidence was presented before the Sanhedrin. This was not done at Jesus' trial.

For the testimony of a witness to be considered valid, it must agree in every detail with that of the other witnesses. Once again, this was not the case in Jesus' trial because the witnesses contradicted each other.

The law stated that if the verdict was one of death, a night must elapse before it was carried out, so that the court might have a chance to change its mind and its decision. This law was ignored as well.

Also, before a verdict could be delivered, every member of the Sanhedrin was to give his verdict, one at a time. They were to start with the youngest and poll every member up through the eldest. Here we see that the high priest delivered the verdict and the members were not polled.

The law forbade asking leading questions of the accused. Yet, the record shows that this law was broken as well.

> They all asked, "Are you then the Son of God?"
> He replied, "You are right in saying I am" (verse 70).

As if all this were not enough, they condemned Jesus right then without polling the members. "Then they said, 'Why do we need any more testimony? We have heard it from his own lips' " (verse 71).

At every step, the trial of Jesus by the Sanhedrin was a fraud! Every law protecting the rights of the accused was violated. Jesus was denied every right afforded Him by law.

Realizing that the Sanhedrin could not execute anyone, the leaders decided to take Jesus to Pilate, the Roman governor. Before the Sanhedrin, Jesus had been charged with blasphemy. This was a religious charge and would mean nothing to Pilate. So the leaders changed the charge when they came before Pilate. They now accused Jesus of subverting the nation, opposing the payment of taxes, and claiming to be a king (see Luke 23:2). They knew they had to come up with political charges or Pilate would not listen. They knew these charges were unfounded—and so did Pilate—but in an attempt to please the Sanhedrin, Pilate played along.

As Pilate examined Jesus, he could find no cause to condemn Him. So when he learned that Jesus was from Galilee, he sent Him to Herod, because Galilee was Herod's jurisdiction.

Herod had long wanted to see Jesus. He was intrigued by the stories of healings and other miraculous acts. So Herod tried to get Jesus to perform a miracle, but Jesus said not a word. He didn't even try to defend Himself or to answer His accusers.

Herod was so frustrated by this that he taunted Jesus. He dressed Him in an elegant robe and mocked Him. Having thus satisfied his sick need to humiliate his adversary, Herod then sent Jesus back to Pilate.

Jesus' return frustrated Pilate. He wanted an easy way out. Since it was the custom for the governor to release a prisoner every year during the Passover, he thought this might be a good opportunity to get out of this unpleasant business. He held in custody a man named Barabbas.

Barabbas was a bandit and a murderer. Again we turn to Luke for the story: "Pilate called together the chief priests, the rulers and the people, and said to them, 'You brought me this man as one who was inciting the people to rebellion. I have examined him in your presence and have found no basis for your charges against him. Neither has Herod, for he sent him back to us; as you can see, he has done nothing to deserve death. Therefore, I will punish him and then release him' " (verses 13–16). This was not what the crowd wanted. The priests incited them to near riot conditions. They cried out for Barabbas to be released and for Jesus to be crucified. Pilate did not want to execute an innocent man, but eventually the anger of the crowd won the day.

> Wanting to release Jesus, Pilate appealed to them again. But they kept shouting, "Crucify him! Crucify him!"
>
> For the third time he spoke to them: "Why? What crime has this man committed? I have found in him no grounds for the death penalty. Therefore I will have him punished and then release him."
>
> But with loud shouts they insistently demanded that he be crucified, and their shouts prevailed. So Pilate decided to grant their demand. He released the man who had been thrown into prison for insurrection and murder, the one they asked for, and surrendered Jesus to their will (verses 20–25).

Jesus allowed Himself to be arrested on trumped-up charges, illegally tried, and condemned to die by governmental officials who were convinced of His innocence. Why did the Son of God allow all of this to happen? Why did He endure it? Because Jesus longed for you to be restored to the loving arms of your Father! He wanted this so badly that He was willing to make the ultimate sacrifice for you. He endured it all because of His great love for you. G. K. Chesterton wrote, "All men matter. You matter. I matter. It's the hardest thing in theology to believe."

Jesus endured the ignominy of His illegal arrest and trial to demonstrate to you that you really do matter to Him. You matter so much, in fact, that He endured the ultimate sacrifice so that you could be restored to the loving arms of your Father!

In June 1940, the fate of Great Britain was in doubt. Nazi bombs threatened to destroy the British Empire. Only the Royal Air Force stood between Hitler and the people of England. Their heroic efforts saved the country, but at a terrible cost.

One young airman, Pilot Officer V. A. Rosenwarne, wrote to his mother just before what proved to be his last mission. *The Times of London* published his letter on June 18, 1940. This brave young man wrote, "The universe is so vast and so ageless that the life of one man can only be justified by the measure of his sacrifice."

V. A. Rosenwarne made the ultimate sacrifice for his mother and his country. No greater act of love can be made than to give one's life for another.

Using the measure of Jesus' sacrifice, we must say that His life is more than justified. Jesus endured wrongful arrest; illegal trial; undeserved beatings; humiliation; a painful, ignominious death; and separation from His Father so that we would never need to experience those things. His sacrifice was unthinkable! The benefits of His sacrifice were of immeasurable value. This makes Jesus' life the most significant life the world has ever known.

After Jesus was arrested and tried, He was handed over to the Roman soldiers to be executed. Jesus had already been scourged. Scourging was a horrible experience of torture. The prisoner's back was exposed, and his hands were tied over his head. A strong man usually stood in front of the prisoner with a whip called a cat-o'-nine-tails. This instrument had nine leather straps, each having a razor-sharp object attached to the end.

The soldier would whip the prisoner in such a way that the nine sharp objects lodged themselves in the prisoner's back. Then the soldier would pull the whip, and the nine sharp points ripped through the skin, producing horizontal tears in the flesh. This was done thirty-nine times, usually with thirteen stokes on the chest and twenty-six on the back. Many victims died during this process.

Jesus' body was little more than raw, bleeding meat! He was seriously weakened by loss of blood. But now the soldiers took a wreath woven of one-inch thorns and drove it deeply into His head. They covered Him with an old purple robe and mocked Him as the "King" of the Jews.

They put a reed in His hand as a "scepter" and then took it and struck Him on the head with it.

The guards spat in the face of the Son of God and bowed before Him in mock worship. They beat Him with their fists and then took Him out to be crucified.

Crucifixions followed a fairly fixed procedure. The criminal had to carry his own cross to the place of execution. Four soldiers boxed in the criminal, with one walking in front of the condemned carrying a board stating the crime he had been convicted of. Later, that board was nailed to the cross.

The soldiers always took the longest route to the place of execution, following every possible street and lane so that as many people as possible could see. Jesus was so weakened by the experience that He was unable to carry His cross all the way to the place of execution. "As they led him away, they seized Simon from Cyrene, who was on his way in from the country, and put the cross on him and made him carry it behind Jesus. A large number of people followed him, including women who mourned and wailed for him. Jesus turned and said to them, 'Daughters of Jerusalem, do not weep for me; weep for yourselves and for your children' " (verses 26–28).

When they reached the place of crucifixion, the cross was placed flat on the ground. The prisoner was stretched upon it, and his hands and feet nailed to it.

New Testament scholar William Barclay tells us that between the prisoner's legs was a ledge of wood called the saddle, which took the weight of the body when the cross was raised upright. Otherwise the nails might rip through the flesh of the hands. When the cross was lifted up and set in its socket, the criminal was left to die.

The cross was not usually tall. In most cases it was shaped like the letter "T," rather than the traditional shape we see in pictures today. Sometimes prisoners hung on the cross for as long as a week, slowly dying of hunger and of thirst, and sometimes suffering to the point of actual madness.

As Jesus carried His cross through the streets of Jerusalem, Simon of Cyrene happened upon this grisly parade. Simon had come from Africa to celebrate the Passover in Jerusalem. He happened to be in the wrong place at the wrong time. When Jesus, weakened by the beatings, fell beneath the load of the cross, the Roman guard compelled Simon to carry the cross for our Savior.

At the time, Simon must have resented it. He must have hated the Romans and hated this "criminal" whose cross he was being forced to carry. No doubt, when he got to Golgotha, he threw the cross down on the ground and stepped aside.

Whatever happened to Simon? Simon, his wife, and his sons were all converted to Christianity. Simon is listed as the father of Alexander and Rufus. They and their mother were known well by the church in Rome.

It also appears that Simon was among those men from Antioch who sent Paul and Barnabas out on their first missionary journey. Simon, a man who had come to eat the Passover lamb, instead met the Lamb of God and carried His cross. The event forever changed Simon's life, as well as the lives of his family.

Two other men, both criminals, were also led out with him to be executed. When they came to the place called the Skull, there they crucified him, along with the criminals—one on his right, the other on his left. Jesus said, "Father, forgive them, for they do not know what they are doing." And they divided up his clothes by casting lots.

The people stood watching, and the rulers even sneered at him. They said, "He saved others; let him save himself if he is the Christ of God, the Chosen One."

The soldiers also came up and mocked him. They offered him wine vinegar and said, "If you are the king of the Jews, save yourself" (verses 32–37).

Jesus hung on the cross, dying in agony. A group of women whose hearts were merciful attended every execution and offered the criminals a drink of drugged wine to ease the pain. Jesus refused the mixture.

The religious leaders of the day taunted Jesus as He hung on the cross. Like unruly juveniles, they danced before the cross and hurled insults at the Son of God. "If You really are the Son of God, come down and save Yourself. Then we'll believe You."

The fact is, it is because Jesus did not come down from the cross that we believe in Him. The death of Jesus was absolutely necessary, and the reason was this: Jesus came to reconcile us to the Father. Our sin had separated us from our Father, but Jesus made the necessary sacrifice to return us to His loving arms. If He had refused to endure the cross and had come down, it would have meant that there was a limit to God's love—that there was something which that love was not prepared to suffer for men, that there was a line beyond which it would not go. But Jesus went the whole way and died at the cross, and this means that there is literally no limit to God's love.

There is nothing in the whole of the universe that His love is not prepared to suffer for you, and there is nothing, not even death on a cross, that it will refuse to bear for you. Look at the Cross and hear Jesus cry, "My love for you is so great that I am willing to make a sacrifice this large for your benefit. I will bear every suffering the world has to offer. My love is a love that will stop at nothing to return you to the loving arms of your Father."

Such love is irresistible! How can anyone look such love in the face and reject it?

One of the criminals who was executed with Jesus looked into the face of love and embraced it. Two thieves were crucified with Jesus that day. One hurled insults at Jesus, but the other rebuked his fellow thief. Then he looked at Jesus and made a request of Him:

> Then he said, "Jesus, remember me when you come into your kingdom."
> Jesus answered him, "I tell you the truth, today you will be with me in paradise" (verses 42, 43).

This man looked into the face of love and asked for mercy. Love looked back and granted mercy. Love extended a promise of eternal life.

Verse forty-three has been mistranslated to suggest that the thief and Jesus went to Paradise that day. This is not true because the thief did not die that day, but was left on the cross over the Sabbath. The soldiers broke his legs to prevent him from running away, but he was very much alive throughout that day.

In addition, Jesus did not go to Paradise that day, either. He said so three days later, after His resurrection. He said that He had not yet ascended to the Father, so we know that He had not yet gone to Paradise (see John 20:17).

In essence, what Jesus said to the repentant thief was this: "Today I tell you the truth, you will be with Me in Paradise." If we may paraphrase, Jesus was saying, "Today, when all seems so bleak and lost and hopeless— today, when it seems that the forces of evil have triumphed—today, when you and I are hanging on a cross—I tell you today, that your request will be granted. You will be with Me in Paradise." That very day, the thief received the promise of Paradise with Jesus, a promise that will be fulfilled when Jesus returns to claim him and everyone else who embraces His love.

Luke tells us what happened next:

> It was now about the sixth hour, and darkness came over the whole land until the ninth hour, for the sun stopped shining. And the curtain of the temple was torn in two. Jesus called out with a loud voice, "Father, into your hands I commit my spirit." When he had said this, he breathed his last.
>
> The centurion, seeing what had happened, praised God and said, "Surely this was a righteous man" (verses 44–47).

In John's Gospel we learn that as Jesus breathed His last He cried, "It is finished!" (John 19:30). In the original text the words *it is* do not appear. Only the word *finished* is written. This was a cry of victory—a cry of triumph! Jesus had completed His work of reconciliation. His work of love was complete. His sacrifice paid the price for your sins and grants you eternal life.

Thus Luke ends his telling of the story of the greatest sacrifice of love the world has ever seen. Jesus placed Himself at great peril for your sake. He surrendered His body—His very life—to return you to the loving arms of the Father.

The other day I was reading from a book by Talbert Shaw, *East of Eden*. In that little book I found a wonderful story of sacrifice.

Shaw tells of a white teacher who was watching one of her students, a black boy, who was unable to catch a football. The passes were not difficult to catch, but John dropped each pass. She asked him why he was unable to catch even the easiest of passes, and the boy responded, "I can't, ma'am, because I am on dialysis."

John's reply so touched his teacher that she made a decision that had lifelong consequences. After long discussions with her family, this teacher decided to give one of her kidneys to John.

Tests proved that she was a viable donor, so this white woman gave a part of her body to a black student who was dying from kidney failure. The surgeries were successful, and John has a new kidney—and a new life.

Shaw writes, "John and his teacher are back in school. As she watches him play football and catch balls with unagonizing ease, as he interacts with students without pain, as he holds up his hands in her class to answer a question, his teacher, his 'savior,' looks at him as an extension of her life."

Christ gave more than just a kidney; He gave His very life so that you might become an extension of His life. His sacrifice affords us a life of uninterrupted, unfettered fellowship with the Father.

What is your response to such great love? Only a gift of love from you will be appropriate. Respond with your heart. Give Him your love.

Chapter Thirteen

What Gives You Hope Today?

Based on Luke 24

Darkness. Pitch black, darkness covered the earth the day Jesus died. Not just the darkness that occurred with the blotting out of the light of the sun at Jesus' death, but the darkness that comes when the hopes and dreams of men and women have been destroyed.

There is no darkness like the darkness that comes when there is no hope.

When I was a chaplain for a psychiatric hospital, I had the opportunity to visit with a young woman who had attempted suicide. I asked her what had driven her to that point—what had caused her to resort to so desperate and dangerous a recourse. Her answer was, "I just felt that there was no hope. Things were so bad that there was no hope that they could ever get better. It seemed to me that all the world was darkness, and I wanted out."

Chuck Colson writes of several Christian leaders who met with President Borja of Ecuador. The purpose of their visit was to discuss Prison Fellowship International's ministry in Ecuadorian prisons. To begin the meeting, President Borja told the story of his own imprisonment, which had taken place several years before he was elected president. Borja had been active in the fight for democracy in Ecuador. When a military crackdown ensued, he was arrested and imprisoned without benefit of a trial.

He was thrown into a cold dungeon with no windows and no light. It was so dark there that he could not see his own hand when he held it directly in front of his face. He sat for three days in that darkness, the kind of darkness that can drive a person mad. Borja felt he could endure the darkness no longer.

But just when he was at the end of his rope, someone opened the huge steel door to his cell. Without saying a word, the person stepped into the cell and worked on something in the opposite corner from where Borja sat. Then the individual left, and the door closed.

As the minutes passed, Borja wondered what had just happened. But his questions were answered when suddenly the room filled with light. Someone, perhaps at the risk of his own life, had repaired the broken light fixture and connected it to electricity. President Borja said, "From that moment, my imprisonment had meaning because at least I could see."

Darkness brings fear, despair, loneliness, and hopelessness, while light brings comfort and hope. Our hearts long for light. Jesus declares Himself to be the Light, thus fulfilling our heart's desire.

We can only imagine how dark things must have felt for the disciples when Jesus was crucified. Friday night must have been the worst time in their lives. They had invested their lives, their reputations, their futures, and their fortunes in the Man from Galilee. Their hopes and dreams for a better tomorrow all rested on Jesus.

While Jesus was alive, the disciples felt a fulfillment they had never known before. Before Jesus, their hearts had been vacuums. That was changed when they met Jesus. He filled their empty hearts with love, forgiveness, pity, hope, and new purposes for living. But now that He was dead, their hearts were once again empty. Their hopes and dreams were dashed, and there was nothing left but darkness. Darkness is the absence of hope.

After Jesus died, Joseph of Arimathea, a member of the Sanhedrin, asked for Jesus' body. Because he was a member of the Sanhedrin, and because the vote of that judicial body was unanimous for crucifixion, either Joseph was not notified of the meeting or he had abstained. It is more likely that he was known to be sympathetic to Jesus and was therefore excluded from that particular meeting.

Once Jesus had been crucified, Joseph asked for His body so that he might give it a proper burial. This was risky because all of his peers were very much opposed to Jesus—so much so that they had participated in facilitating His death. But Joseph bravely asked Pilate for permission to bury Jesus' body. He wrapped the body in linen and laid it in his own tomb, a hollowed out place in a rock.

Because the Sabbath was about to begin, there was no time to completely follow the custom of preparing the body for burial with spices. So Joseph and the others left Jesus there and rolled a large stone across the opening to the tomb. The women who had followed Jesus to the place of His execution went home to prepare the spices and then rested on the Sabbath. Their plan was to return to the tomb on Sunday morning to prepare the body for final burial.

That Sabbath was a dark, dreary day for those who had placed their confidence in Jesus. A vast emptiness consumed their hearts.

Sabbath had always been a special time for them. They had always been able to lay aside the cares and concerns of the week to focus on God their Creator. Every Sabbath they went to the synagogue, or better yet, to the temple, to recite the psalms, sing, witness the sacrifices, and pray. It was always a wonderful experience for them—a time of hope and joy and celebration.

But on this Sabbath there was no hope or joy and certainly no celebrating for the disciples. Jesus, the One they believed to be the Messiah, lay in a borrowed tomb. All their hopes were buried in that tomb. When hope leaves, darkness enters.

However, those who trust in Christ are never completely in darkness. Even when it appears that the light has been forever vanquished, in the heart of every true believer remains the tiniest flicker of light. And that small light is enough to allow hope to live.

Years ago, a friend of mine was visiting New York City when he was caught in an elevator during a power failure. The elevator stopped between floors and the lights went out, leaving the passengers in total darkness.

You know how it is when strangers get into an elevator. They never talk! Rarely do they even make eye contact. But when the lights went out on that elevator, all seven strangers talked at once. Everyone was frantic.

After the initial panic, my friend remembered that he had a tiny flashlight in his pocket. When he turned it on, the fear dissipated. They were stuck in that elevator for nearly an hour, but as long as the flashlight worked, they told jokes, laughed, and even sang. Light brings hope and hope brings light. Hope banishes fear.

The disciples had forgotten that Jesus had predicted His own death. But with the prediction of death was also a prediction of resurrection. If they had remembered this, the darkness they experienced that Sabbath would have given way to light.

Luke tells us what happened on Sunday morning:

> On the first day of the week, very early in the morning, the women took the spices they had prepared and went to the tomb. They found the stone rolled away from the tomb, but when they entered, they did not find the body of the Lord Jesus. While they were wondering about this, suddenly two men in clothes that gleamed like lightning stood beside them. In their fright the women bowed down with their faces to the ground, but the men said to them, "Why do you look for the living among the dead? He is not here; he has risen! Remember how he told you, while he was still with you in Galilee: 'The Son of Man must be delivered into the hands of sinful men, be crucified and on the third day be raised again.' " Then they remembered his words (Luke 24:1–8).

When the women found the empty tomb and were reminded of Jesus' words, they were filled with hope; darkness gave way to light.

The passage we have just read describes what is likely the most important event in the history of the universe—the resurrection of Jesus. This story is the heart of all Christian theology. There are those who would reject this story. They say that the stories of miracles and of the Resurrection are actually nothing more than allegory—fictitious stories with wonderful lessons for life.

I submit to you that if Jesus Christ is not raised from the dead, then you and I have absolutely no hope and all the world is darkness. However, if Christ is raised from the dead, then we have hope, for we, too, can live again. Luke tells us that the good news is this: The tomb of Jesus is empty.

"When they came back from the tomb, they told all these things to the Eleven and to all the others. It was Mary Magdalene, Joanna, Mary the mother of James, and the others with them who told this to the apostles. But they did not believe the women, because their words seemed to them like nonsense. Peter, however, got up and ran to the tomb. Bending over, he saw the strips of linen lying by themselves, and he went away, wondering to himself what had happened" (verses 9–12). When the women told the disciples what they had seen, the disciples did not believe them. They went to see for themselves, but they, too, found an empty tomb. Peter wondered what this meant. You, too, must decide what this means for you. What does Jesus' empty tomb mean for your life?

Some declare that it is impossible for one to be raised from the dead, and so Jesus could not have risen.

But consider this. The story of the Resurrection was heralded throughout Jerusalem. If any could have refuted that story, they would have done so then. But none did. Why? Because the tomb was empty!

Some suggest that Jesus only fainted on the cross, and that when He was placed in the cool recesses of the tomb He revived and then released Himself.

For that to be true Jesus, after hanging nine hours on the cross and being placed in a tomb for more than two days with no food and no water, would have had to be so revived that He was able to get up and walk on wounded feet and with pierced hands push away a stone that took many men to move. Then, after having pushed away that stone, Jesus would have had to overpower armed Roman soldiers and escape.

It is easier for me to believe that He rose from the dead!

Some say the friends of Jesus came and stole His body away so that they might claim He had risen from the dead. But that would mean that they would have to overpower the Roman soldiers and steal the body of Christ. It would also mean that they were willing to die for what they knew was untrue. It would mean that they were willing to be crucified, thrown to wild animals, endure punishment and torture for what they knew all along to be a lie. Most people will not die for what they know to be truth, let alone for what they know to be a lie.

Galileo, through his studies, learned that the earth revolved around the sun and wrote of his findings. But when the church ordered him to renounce his teachings as heresy or face execution, Galileo recanted. He was not willing to die for what he knew to be true, much less for a lie. The disciples knew the resurrection of Jesus was not a lie, and that is why they were willing to die for Him.

At the center of our faith stands an empty tomb. Jesus Christ is risen! He is the Lord of life, and He is the Lord of death! Because of that, you and I have hope.

Light has invaded the darkness, and fear is vanquished! Our hope is based on the resurrected Lord!

Among the Jews of Jerusalem, the dawn of the Day of Atonement was eagerly awaited. A watchman stood on the walls watching for sunrise. When he saw the first rays, he would shout, "Light! Light! I have seen the light!"

That Friday, Jesus' death left His followers in darkness darker than a moonless night. They believed they would never see the light again. Those who mourned His passing placed His body in a borrowed tomb and then retreated into darkness.

Few experiences of life are any darker than the experience of mourning. As a pastor and a chaplain, I have conducted hundreds of funerals. I have watched as loved ones mourned the deceased. I have listened as they wept over their great loss. For them, the world seems dark.

But because Jesus died and rose again, we have hope even in the midst of darkness. Because of Jesus' experience, those who trust in Him will live again.

The resurrection of Christ brings light to those who mourn in darkness. Like the ancient watchman on the walls of Jerusalem awaiting the dawn of the Day of Atonement, we cry "Light! Light! I have seen the light!" We do so because of the resurrection of Jesus.

Hope is reborn because of an empty tomb. Resurrection swallows up death in glorious victory, and light invades the province of darkness.

Perhaps you have experienced this. Even in the midst of the darkness of mourning, you retain a flicker of light because of the hope you have in the resurrection.

Several years ago there was a well-known television circus show that included a Bengal tiger act. The show was done "live" before a large audience.

One evening, during a routine performance, the lights went out! The tiger trainer was locked inside the cage with the tigers, armed only with a whip and a small kitchen chair. The lights remained off for twenty or thirty long, dark seconds. The tigers could see the trainer, but the trainer could not see the tigers. Finally, the lights came on, and the trainer calmly finished the performance.

In an interview afterward, they asked the trainer how he felt knowing that the tigers could see him, but that he could not see them. He said that at first he experienced a cold chill and feared for his life. But then he remembered that the tigers did not know that he could not see them. He said, "I just kept cracking my whip and talking to them until the lights came on. And they never knew I could not see them as well as they could see me."

When death comes and your heart is broken, you find yourself, at least temporarily, in darkness. At that moment, even though you are unable to see, the hope of resurrection enables you to continue to fight tigers in the dark. Hope gives you the courage to go on living when you've lost your reason to live.

According to legend, the sphinx was a creature that was half woman and half lion. The legend stated that the sphinx used to lie stretched upon a rock at the entrance to a city. When people approached, she gave them a riddle. If a traveler could not answer the riddle, she would push the traveler off the cliff.

The riddle was, "What goes on four legs in the morning, two legs at noon, and three legs at night?" No one could answer the riddle, so they were all pushed over the cliff.

But that changed when Oedipus came along. The sphinx presented the riddle to Oedipus and he gave the answer, man. Man crawls on all fours in the morning of his years. In the noontime of life, man walks upon two legs. And in the evening of life, man walks with a cane.

The legend tells us that when the sphinx heard the answer to the riddle, she leaped to her death. Death has been the great riddle that no one could answer. But Jesus answered the riddle and defeated that last great enemy, death. Hope and light have returned because of our resurrected Lord. Every Christian teaching hangs on this event. If Christ is not raised from the dead, everything we believe is a sham. If Christ is not raised, we have no hope. This life is all that exists. The grave is the last chapter for everyone.

But if Jesus was indeed raised from the grave, life has meaning, and even in death we find hope.

In the book *Dorothy L. Sayers: A Careless Rage for Life*, we read,

> "And the third day he rose again." What are we to make of this? One thing is certain: if [Jesus] were God and nothing else, his immortality means nothing to us; if he was man and no more, his death is no more important than yours or mine. But if he really was both God and man, then when the man Jesus died, God died too; and when the God Jesus rose from the dead, man rose too, because they were one and the same person. . . . There is the essential doctrine, of which the whole elaborate structure of Christian faith and morals is only the logical consequence. Now we may call that doctrine exhilarating, or we may call it devastating; we may call it revelation, or we may call it rubbish; but if we call it dull, then words have no meaning at all.

Christ rose from the grave! His death and resurrection change everything. When the women who visited Jesus' grave that Sunday morning saw that Jesus had been resurrected, they could not contain their joy! They ran to tell the disciples. Intuitively, these women realized that this was the greatest news the world had ever received! Light had pierced the darkness, and hope returned.

But the disciples did not believe the women. They wanted to hope, but were cautious, not wanting to have hope dashed again. So the disciples had to check the story out for themselves. When they arrived at the tomb, they found that it was empty, just as the women had said.

At first, they were confused, not really daring to hope.

Later that same day two of the men decided to travel from Jerusalem to the village of Emmaus, a journey of about seven miles. As you might imagine, these men spoke only of recent events as they walked together, neither understanding what it all meant. Their hearts were heavy with grief, their eyes unable to see for the darkness of mourning.

As they traveled, a third man joined them and asked what they had been talking about. The two men were surprised that anyone could imagine talking about anything other than the death of Jesus. So they told the stranger of their disappointment at the death of Jesus and their confusion at the empty tomb.

What these men did not know was that the stranger was, in fact, Jesus. He had purposefully hidden His identity from them. "He said to them, 'How foolish you are, and how slow of heart to believe all that the prophets have spoken! Did not the Christ have to suffer these things and then enter his glory?' And beginning with Moses and all the Prophets, he explained to them what was said in all the Scriptures concerning himself" (verses 25–27). Jesus explained from Scripture the plan of salvation. He explained that the Christ had to suffer and to die so that man might be saved. Jesus told them that the Messiah had come to pay the penalty for sin so that human beings could have the greatest longings of their heart fulfilled—the longing for deep, uninterrupted intimacy with God.

As He spoke to these men, they felt as though someone had lit a candle in their dark hearts. The light of hope began to flicker once again.

The two men were so thrilled by what the Stranger said that when they arrived at their destination they invited the Man to eat with them. Once the meal was prepared, they asked Him to bless the food, and it was then that they recognized Jesus. As soon as they recognized Him, Jesus disappeared from their sight.

The Scripture says, "They asked each other, 'Were not our hearts burning within us while he talked with us on the road and opened the Scriptures to us?' " (verse 32). This experience lit a candle in their hearts. That candle grew to a great bonfire. Hope returned, and their eyes were opened. They could feel the warmth as they recognized that Jesus, the risen Christ, was the fulfillment of their hearts' desire. Hope sprang eternal!

The men forgot about the meal, ran back to Jerusalem, and told the others that they had seen Jesus. They shared with them the teachings Jesus had given them from Scripture. While they were still telling the story, Jesus appeared in the midst of them and said, "Peace be with you."

The disciples were frightened and thought they were seeing a ghost, but Jesus showed them His hands and His feet and encouraged them to touch Him so that they might know that He was not a ghost, but flesh and blood.

They were so confused! How could this be?

Jesus gave another Bible study, sharing the scriptures that foretold all that the Messiah must endure and why. He told them that their job now was to be the witnesses of these things and that God would give them power to do this work.

Then it was time for Jesus to leave. "When he had led them out to the vicinity of Bethany, he lifted up his hands and blessed them. While he was blessing them, he left them and was taken up into heaven. Then they worshiped him and returned to Jerusalem with great joy. And they stayed continually at the temple, praising God" (verses 50–53). The darkness of crucifixion turned into the light of resurrection, and with that light came joy. The disciples were filled with joy and praised God.

The resurrection of Jesus continues to bring hope today. Because Jesus was raised from the dead, all those who love Him will be raised from death to life. The apostle Paul, writing to believers in the church at Thessalonica, said:

> Brothers, we do not want you to be ignorant about those who fall asleep, or to grieve like the rest of men, who have no hope. We believe that Jesus died and rose again and so we believe that God will bring with Jesus those who have fallen asleep in him. According to the Lord's own word, we tell you that we who are still alive, who are left till the coming of the Lord, will certainly not precede those who have fallen asleep. For the Lord himself will come down from heaven, with a loud command, with the voice of the archangel and with the trumpet call of God, and the dead in Christ will rise first. After that, we who are still alive and are left will be caught up together with them in the clouds to meet the Lord in the air. And so we will be with the Lord forever (1 Thessalonians 4:13–17).

Notice what Paul says. He says that because Jesus died and rose again, so too will those who have died "in Him" rise again. The resurrection of the dead is sealed because of what Christ has done. His resurrection guarantees that even though those who love Jesus may die, they will rise again, just as Christ rose again.

When did Paul say this would happen? "The Lord himself will come down from heaven, with a loud command, with the voice of the archangel and with the trumpet call of God." The dead will rise at the second coming of Jesus.

Also notice that Paul tells us why Jesus will come again to collect to Himself those who died in Him and those who live in Him. He does it so that "we will be with the Lord forever."

The longing of your heart is to be with Jesus. That same longing—a longing to be with you—fills the heart of Jesus. He is coming again to raise the dead to life and to bring the living saints to be with Him in heaven so that He might fulfill the desires of your heart and of His. He is coming so that we might be with the Lord forever.

In John's Gospel, Jesus tells us, " 'Do not let your hearts be troubled. Trust in God; trust also in me. In my Father's house are many rooms; if it were not so, I would have told you. I am going there to prepare a place for you. And if I go and prepare a place for you, I will come back and take you to be with me that you also may be where I am' " (John 14:1–3).

Why is Jesus coming back? He is coming back so that you can be wherever He is.

Sin separated you from God; it left you incomplete, defective. But Jesus came to make you whole. He paid the penalty for your sin, bridged the gap between you and the Father, and now has promised to return for you. You will never be separated from Him again. Not even death can keep us from Jesus, for He is "the resurrection and the life."

This is your heart's great desire—to see the face of God and be with Jesus forever. Jesus offers today to fulfill your heart's desire. What prevents you from saying "yes" to His gracious offer? Fulfill your heart's desire by praying this simple prayer:

Dear Jesus, I long to have a relationship of intimacy with You. I realize that my sin has prevented such a relationship; therefore,

I confess my sin before You today and ask to be forgiven.

You have promised to forgive me whenever I ask, so I trust that You have done as You have promised. I thank You for forgiving my sin today.

I acknowledge that You are the Son of God and that You died for my sins. I also believe that You rose from the grave and that You live today, interceding on my behalf before God the Father.

I ask for the free gift of eternal life made possible by Your sacrifice. Since You have promised that You will never turn anyone away who calls on Your name, I now give thanks for salvation. I believe that I will live forever with You.

Draw me closer every day. Help me to live in Your love, acceptance, and forgiveness every moment of my life. I ask You to be the Lord of my life, guiding and directing my every decision.

I give You my love, Lord Jesus. Because I love You, I praise You and promise to worship only You. I give You my worship and my obedience as a response to Your love for me.

I look forward to the day of Your return. On that day I will live in uninterrupted fellowship with You.

Thank You for loving me. And thank You for seeing my heart's desire. You alone can satisfy that desire. I claim Your satisfaction of my heart's desire today. Amen.

If you prayed this simple prayer, you can rest assured that you belong to Jesus. You will live forever with the only One who can satisfy your heart's desire.

Live in obedience to Him today. As you do, you will discover what so many others have found—that Jesus truly is your heart's desire.

Other books by Mike Tucker include:

Journal of a Lonely God

Author and *Faith For Today* speaker Mike Tucker probes the stories in Genesis about the Creator's dealings with Adam, Abraham, and Isaac to reveal a God who is reaching out to His creation with an invitation to be with Him.
0-8163-2071-3. Paperback.
US$9.99, Can$14.99.

Jesus, Your Heart's Desire

Pastor Mike Tucker of Faith for Today Ministries shares glimpses of Jesus' love and concern for people as shown in stories from the Gospel of Luke.
0-8163-2102-7. Paperback.
US$1.99, Can$2.69.

Order from your ABC by calling **1-800-765-6955,** or get online and shop our virtual store at **www.AdventistBookCenter.com**.

- Read a chapter from your favorite book
- Order online
- Sign up for email notices on new products

Prices subject to change without notice.